MW01037396

SECRETS OF
SUCCESS

SECRETS OF
SUCCESS

INSIGHTS FROM MEGAN RAPINOE'S
WORLD-CLASS SOCCER CAREER

MEG LINEHAN

Skyhorse Publishing

Contents

Introduction

"We're here, we're ready. Everyone's ready to do more?"

Megan Rapinoe never hid who she is. Until 2019, she was definitely one of the more popular women's soccer players in America, but she wasn't exactly a household name. She wasn't an athlete who had yet elevated to the "one name is all it takes" level of recognition—a LeBron, a Serena, a Messi. She might not be on that first name level yet, but Pinoe isn't too far off.

Before Rapinoe, there was a handful of women's soccer players who achieved some notable level of mainstream status, usually due to the profile boost of a World Cup, and better yet, a World Cup win. Mia Hamm was the star in 1999, when the tournament was on home soil, but Brandi Chastain provided an iconic image as well thanks to her penalty kick celebration. Then there was Abby Wambach, who overtook Hamm's international goalscoring record, Carli Lloyd, who astonished in the 2015 World Cup final, and Alex Morgan, who became the face of the program for a number of years.

In the summer of 2019, though, Megan Rapinoe transcended the sport in a way no player ever had before. So many storylines and factors converged into one month, both on and off the field. The United States women's national team sued their own federation for equal pay, equal investment, and equal respect. Rapinoe made headlines earlier in her career, after she kneeled in solidarity with Colin Kaepernick and other athletes to bring attention to police brutality and racism. The national team was trying to win back-to-back World Cups, even as the international competition grew stronger, and the 2019 tournament was widely expected to be one of the toughest in the competition's history. The US national team was already linked to the political discourse as well—thanks to larger conversations about equality and women's reproductive rights in America.

As Rapinoe and the team took off for Europe, they offered some alternative vision of what America is, and could be—strong women united with a single purpose. The best in the world, ready to live up to FIFA's motto for the tournament: Dare to Shine.

The team did shine. They did win back-to-back World Cups; Rapinoe led the way with six goals, including the game-winners in three of the four knock-out stage matches.

And as much as Rapinoe has been celebrated for those accomplishments on the field, when she returned to the States, bringing a couple of extra awards back with her, she found herself at the center of the American media—not answering soccer questions, but talking about politics, about equal pay, about how people could be better.

As usual, Megan Rapinoe was unlike pretty much every other player that had come before her. Of course, the way she approached her newfound fame was unlike any other as well.

Megan Rapinoe spent a few months following the World Cup simply asking for people to "do something, do anything." She asked that of every single person, regardless of the amount of power or influence they had, though she paid particular attention to all of the people she encountered who did have more power, who had larger platforms, such as she did herself.

An analysis of the success of Megan Rapinoe reveals one simple belief: that every single person has the power to change their world through their own actions. The impact may be small—it may only extend to a family member, a friend, the community. For some, that impact may be large. But if everyone buys into this belief, if everyone believes that there is the possibility of becoming better together, then it works. But it has to start with the belief that this is even possible.

While her ideas are simple, they do require a radical shift away from cynicism. Temporary frustrations are part of the daily existence—but giving up completely isn't an option. Believing you have to be in it for yourself isn't an option. Nihilism and scarcity are only the end products of fear.

Rapinoe was always willing to share her mind, but that willingness is also key to seeing the evolution she herself went through throughout her entire life, and the past decade in particular, to reach her general philosophy. Thanks to the nature of professional sports, she never truly lacked a platform and constantly faced expectations to serve as a role model. But Rapinoe played with those expectations throughout her career, and over the course of the last few years, changed how she's used her platform for her own purposes.

It's crucial to note Rapinoe's evolution. Her journey has been messy, but she has embraced that messiness. She has doubted her own methods. She has questioned herself. She has sometimes been loud, even without always being able to dive into an issue with the expertise of a more-involved activist. She has learned along the way, from all levels. Even as others look to her as an inspiration, she makes sure those conversations go in both directions.

From early childhood to her first call-up with the national team through the 2019 World Cup and beyond, Rapinoe's been influenced by her community, her family, her teammates, friends, activists, movements. Through her willingness to protest, her work on equal pay, and her speeches, she's expanded on how she intends to use her platform to hopefully, eventually, undo the very system that decided her voice should be more important than others.

With each chapter, focusing on the various eras of her life and the issues she has become involved in, there are additional concepts to round out what Rapinoe's trying to accomplish, and lessons that can work for anyone.

"You're damn sure gonna stand up for other people, always."

First takeaway after analyzing Rapinoe's style: The journey will shape you, but never forget where you came from and your fundamental values.

Being kind should not be a radical concept, but Rapinoe was raised to find self-worth not in popularity or her performance on the field, but in how she interacts with the world. This foundation of standing up for herself, her sister, and others is the early version of her view of the world that is dependent on everyone working cooperatively to protect and support those in their community.

"It wasn't easy for me. But it shouldn't be."

Second takeaway: Be authentic to who you are, even when it's tough.

Rapinoe has never forgotten her hometown of Redding, California, even as her own relationship with it grew more complicated as she grew older, and as she felt more empowered to speak her mind. But she also willingly opened up her horizons and educated herself through other peoples' points of view. Without being willing to learn, it's impossible to become a good ally to others. And above all, being an ally won't be easy work.

"Being gay has shaped my life's view."

Third takeaway: Let your identity guide you.

This examination of Rapinoe's guiding philosophies doesn't exist without her publicly coming out in 2012, and how her queer identity has shaped her values. First and foremost, her willingness to be out provided important visibility, and provided a path for other athletes to follow in her footsteps. But visibility is only the first step.

"It's my responsibility to be an ally for other people."

Fourth takeaway: Your identity and your values must result in solidarity and allyship.

Without Rapinoe's education about LGBTQ issues, she wouldn't have been able to make the leap from her own identity to solidarity with others. But in 2016, she understood that she was part of a larger struggle and decided to join Colin Kaepernick's protest to support his fight, and try to advance the conversation he was trying to have.

"This is who I am, I'm damn proud of it, and hopefully you are too."

Fifth takeaway: Know your worth. If others don't see it, take matters into your own hands.

Rapinoe hasn't just lived by a set of values; she's also made sure to understand her own value—even in a sport that has always been doubted when it comes to revenue or marketability. She's also been confident to know how she wants to be presented to the world, and to say no to those who don't have her best interests in mind.

"We won't accept anything less than equal pay."

Sixth takeaway: Stand your ground on equality, always.

At the same time that Rapinoe has understood her own personal value, she's also always understood the larger value of the US women's national team—and has been involved in the team's fight for equal pay since 2016. She's also always framed the conversation to a larger idea of what equal pay actually looks like; after all, it doesn't exist in a vacuum. It takes equal investment, and equal respect.

"It's every single person's responsibility."

Seventh takeaway: You must do your part to change the world around you.

After her return from the World Cup, it didn't matter if she was speaking to a room full of famous footballers or a camp full of youth players—her message has been constant. Every single person can figure out something they can do to make their own lives, and the people's lives around them, better. That something doesn't have to be large, they don't have to be pushing for large-scale change, but working toward something that they can accomplish to improve their community.

"Do anything. We have incredible power in this room."

Eighth takeaway: Demand accountability from those with power.

Rapinoe has, on some level, been uncomfortable with the amount of attention and awards she's been given since July 2019—simply because she is also willing to understand that this attention is a result of her privilege compared to others. At the same time, this attention granted her power of her own. She can demand accountability from those in power more easily, and she takes that responsibility seriously. She's in the same room as leaders of sport and society and can force them to bear witness to inequalities they would prefer to ignore.

"I think we can move on from losing alone to the belief in winning together."

Ninth takeaway: Use your privilege to lift others up. Throw down your ladders.

Megan Rapinoe's sole goal for her platform is to lift others up onto it, and to put them in front of her. To use her ladders and her privilege. To ensure that she is building on the work that came before, and making sure no one else has to fight the same battles she is fighting now.

"I'm not gonna stand there and pretend like I just did this all this by myself."

Tenth takeaway: Grant recognition to those who paved the way, and let them help show you the way forward.

Rapinoe engaged with larger social movements and conversations with other activists. At an event with Gloria Steinem, she was able to put herself in that larger context with help from an outside source—and someone who had been there before.

Rapinoe didn't need external validation, but she showed that she relies on guidance and feedback from others, in order to help refine what she prioritizes.

"I stand for honesty and for truth."

Eleventh takeaway: Don't listen when people tell you to stay in your lane.

At the same time that Rapinoe tries to be aware of those who came before, she's also tried to look at her own history directly in the eye, and redefine what her own American identity means. She has also always refused to stick to sports, even if her methods have been tested or doubted.

She has never put the burden of trying to be perfect on herself; she has always understood there will be people who won't agree. For as much as she wants to bring people up on her platform, she also understands that there are people who would use it for their own purposes. There's a difference between canceling someone, and not allowing them to co-opt your platform. It's essential to allow the conversation to happen, but keep it moving forward.

"I deserve this."

Twelfth takeaway: Celebrate the wins.

As serious as Rapinoe has been in using her platform responsibly, she has also always embraced joy and humor. She has also set aside external concerns about how to celebrate, especially those that are shaped by concepts of gender. As much as knowing her value has been important to her career, she's also had fun with that exact same concept—and been ready to claim what she deserves.

None of these philosophies work, however, if people are too afraid and willing to give in to looking out for themselves instead of the collective good. They only work if people care. And Rapinoe desperately wants people to care.

She's always made a call to action a central part of her post–World Cup public speaking. After all, her work doesn't end with her—it has to carry on like a ripple effect, as the next people take up the call, then issue their own.

She wants buy-in, and she wants action. And if she doesn't see action, she's ready to hold people accountable, in whatever fashion she needs to in order to get the work done. And there's always work to be done. She's still grappling with the fact that there's no clear finish line, that someone else will have to pick up the fight; she worries that she could be doing more.

But at the end of the day, Megan Rapinoe simply wants to know that everyone is willing to do the work. To win together. To do something, to do anything, if it means making it a little bit better for everyone else.

CHAPTER ONE

The journey will shape you, but never forget where you came from and your fundamental values

"You're damn sure gonna stand up for other people, always."

FROM REDDING, CALIFORNIA, MEGAN RAPINOE was part of a large family growing up—parents Jim and Denise raised seven children. Rapinoe was born on July 5, 1985, along with her fraternal twin, Rachael (who is eleven seconds older than Megan). Her older brother Brian was a major early influence in her life—the reason why both Megan and Rachael picked up a soccer ball.

Brian Rapinoe was eight when he started playing; Denise Rapinoe was the coach of his team. As three-year-olds, Megan and Rachael were on the sidelines, watching, then wanting to play themselves.

A year later, and Brian himself would take them across the street for his own informal training sessions to teach them the game.

Redding is in Northern California, in Shasta County, about 160 miles north of Sacramento, 120 south of the Oregon border. The city was mostly built on the timber industry, but experienced tremendous population growth through the 1970s and into the 1980s, when Rapinoe was born.

Megan and Rachael Rapinoe were the youngest of six siblings; the family was pretty solidly middle class. The twins, thanks to the age gap and being the youngest by a solid five years, spent most of their time together.

"We did everything together," Rapinoe recounted in 2015. "We would build tree forts, if we were doing that, we would play house. We would play baseball against each other all the time… We would go fishing in the creek for crawdads. We kind of just roamed."[1]

The twins grew up as self-identified tomboys. As Rapinoe wrote in 2016, the two of them "grew up playing with the boys. We ran around the mean streets of Redding, California, like wild animals. Basketball. Soccer. Flag football. Street hockey. We did it all. We

---

1   Megan Rapinoe's Story, "One Nation. One Team. 23 Stories." *YouTube*, uploaded by US Soccer, April 29, 2015. https://youtu.be /Su1uuN9Fwok

were rocking bowl cuts, loving life. At the time, I didn't see myself as a 'girl.'I didn't see myself as anything. I was just having a blast."[2]

Sports were formative, but they weren't the only factor in helping to shape Rapinoe's childhood. Her mother, Denise, made sure that the kids never took too much stock in external feedback about how good they might be playing, or how well-liked they were at school.

"My mom … impressed upon me and my twin sister at a very young age, you ain't shit 'cause you're good at sports, you ain't shit 'cause you're popular," Rapinoe said during a speech in 2019.[3] "You're gonna be a good person. You're gonna be kind and you're gonna do the right thing. You're gonna stand up for yourself always, you're gonna stand up for each other always and you're damn sure gonna stand up for other people always."

Even as those values of solidarity were instilled in her (and her sister) from a young age, there weren't really any early signs of the activist she would ultimately turn into when not on the soccer field.

---

2   Rapinoe, Megan. "Tomboys," *The Players' Tribune*, April 7, 2016. www.theplayerstribune.com/en-us/articles/megan-rapinoe-uswnt-soccer-tomboys

3   Rapinoe, Megan. "Megan Rapinoe: 'Lending Your Platform to Others Is Cool'" Transcript of speech provided by *Glamour*, November 12, 2019. www.glamour.com/story/megan-rapinoe-women-of-the-year-speech

"I never grew up thinking about this stuff. I wasn't out in the streets marching as a kid," Rapinoe said.[4] "As my life has unfolded, it's just been that way."

Her older brother Brian introduced her to the game and served as the older sibling she and Rachael could follow around. "Megan and Rachael followed me in some ways," Brian Rapinoe said in 2015.[5] "But I'm really glad they didn't in others."

When the twins were ten, Brian was arrested for bringing meth to school at age fifteen. It was the start of a lifetime battle against drug addiction, one that would also keep him in and out of the prison system for the majority of his adult life. In 2019, Brian was celebrating being able to watch his younger sister at the World Cup at a rehabilitation program, rather than solitary confinement.

"There's no other heartbreak that I've ever been through like that," Rapinoe said in a feature by writer Gwen Oxenham for US Soccer that was released ahead of the 2015 World Cup.[6] "Going through that basically from the age of 10 was really hard. For a long time you blame yourself, you think, 'What can I do,' and you're mad at him, but his addiction is not really about you.

4   Parker, Maggie. "How Soccer Star Megan Rapinoe Remains Hopeful: 'Don't F*** with Us,'" *Parade Magazine*, October 22, 2019. parade.com/940125/maggie_parker/us-womens-soccer-player-megan-rapinoe-self-care-women-empowerment/
5   Oxenham, Gwendolyn. "Pinoe's Biggest Fan," US Soccer, June 14, 2015. www.ussoccer.com/stories/2015/06/pinoes-biggest-fan
6   Ibid.

He's not doing the things that he's doing in order to hurt us—that's just a byproduct. It took me a long time to wrap my head around that."

Soccer became a safe space, not just from middle school gender politics for Rapinoe, but from any potential trouble of following Brian's lead.

Rapinoe has memories of her parents' efforts to keep her brother sober and out of the legal system, and how, at the same time they balanced those concerns with keeping the twins playing, at higher and higher levels.

"While they're dealing with our brother, they're taking us to soccer all the time," Rapinoe said. "Spending all their money on his rehab and our soccer. It's kind of incredible what they were able to do for us."

It was right at this same time that women's soccer in America changed drastically, thanks to a major tournament on home soil—including a couple of important matches that were in California.

As Rapinoe wrote in 2019, the timing of the 1999 World Cup came at a formative time. She was playing soccer, but it wasn't the only sport she was playing. She was good, but not necessarily dedicated. She loved it, but it wasn't a defining presence in her life at that point.

The US women's national team made a splash in the 1996 Olympic Games, winning gold on home soil in Atlanta—and setting up the scale of the 1999 World Cup. But the reach of the team during the 1996 Olympics was completely unlike 1999—the gold medal match wasn't even shown on live television. In 1999, the World Cup was a seismic, formative event for an entire generation—including Rapinoe.

"For the girls growing up now, it's hard to understand just how mind-blowing of a thing this was to see," Rapinoe wrote twenty years later. These games were on television. Stadiums were selling out over the country. "It was just this wave that nobody saw coming."[7]

Rapinoe and her sister went to a game at Stanford during that World Cup, the US national team's semifinal against Brazil. In an atmosphere Rapinoe called "electric," and in front of more than 73,000 people, the United States defeated Brazil 2–0 via goals from Cindy Parlow and Michelle Akers.

Rapinoe's reaction, as she recalled two decades later and having played in a few major World Cup games of her own? "Just, holy shit!"[8]

The visibility of the national team at the 1999 World Cup opened up the doors to actually considering soccer as something more than just a sport she enjoyed.

Now, maybe, the idea that if you can see it, you can be it might be a tired inspirational phrase—but back in 1999, the World Cup created a new wave of players who had

---

7 Rapinoe, Megan. "You Can't Get Rid of Your Girl That Easily," *The Players' Tribune*, June 23, 2019. www.theplayerstribune.com /en-us/articles/megan-rapinoe-united-states-world-cup-youre-not -gonna-get-rid-of-your-girl-that-easily
8 Ibid.

an ultimate goal of playing on the biggest stage of the sport. As Rapinoe noted, she wasn't the only young girl heading home and immediately picking up a ball, with a new dream in mind.

And Rapinoe saw a couple of players in particular as representing the kind of role she could play on a team.

In 2019, she said that her two favorite players were midfielder Kristine Lilly and forward Tiffeny Milbrett. They didn't have the flash of Mia Hamm, or the profile of Michelle Akers. But Rapinoe appreciated their low profile, their creativity, and also their build. They gave her hope that someone smaller could still play at the international level. Lilly and Milbrett played the kind of style that Rapinoe appreciated. And even if they weren't underrated in terms of their overall careers, which she fully admitted, she felt they were a little underrated on that team of '99ers.

Rapinoe would follow in Milbrett's footsteps on the national team, but she also followed Milbrett's path through NCAA college soccer, opting to attend the University of Portland with Rachael on athletic scholarships, as well as continued looks from the US youth national team, including the Under-19 Women's World Cup in 2004.

The new environment proved important for a number of reasons, but it also meant that both Megan and Rachael ended up coming out to each other in college. Megan's college career wasn't an easy one, even as she won a national championship with the Pilots in 2005.

The next year, she tore the anterior cruciate ligament in her left knee part way through her sophomore season. She came back from injury, then tore the same ACL two games into her junior year.

"I know this sounds weird, but getting hurt was one of the best things that ever happened to me," she said in 2009.[9] She said it changed her perspective: from having expectations and a set track of results, to appreciating the work she had to actually put in to achieve those results. As she said, the injury grounded her, but made her stronger as well. The new strength was both mental and physical, and while getting hurt set her back, the injury reframed her entire approach to her career. Ultimately, if she could wave a magic wand and never get hurt, she wouldn't take that offer.

Even while the back-to-back injuries were miserable, the timing of them made her think through soccer as a career in a new way and reaffirmed that it was really what she wanted to do with her life. She earned her first United States senior team call-up after the 2005 NCAA championship, earned her first appearance for the team in July, scored her debut goal by October.

The ACL tears meant she didn't play for the national team at all during 2007 and 2008—taking away her shot at both the 2007 World Cup and 2008 Summer

---

9   "Megan Rapinoe: Twice Removed, But Never Gone," US Soccer, archived. March 4, 2009, accessed via Internet Archive Wayback Machine. web.archive.org/web/20130621222423/http:/www.ussoccer .com/news/other/2009/03/megan-rapinoe-twice-removed-but-never -gone.aspx

Olympics rosters, and it taught her valuable lessons about what was within her control. Toughness, mental or physical, couldn't solve every problem.

"Sometime the best and hardest thing to do is to do nothing and have that sense of patience," Rapinoe said. "This experience really opened my eyes to show me that playing soccer is what I want to do as a career right now."[10]

Being forced to watch her teammates play had made her appreciate the simple act of playing. One ACL tear might have been enough, but a second so shortly after? All it did was solidify her appreciation for her talent, her love of the game.

Rapinoe made her return to the national team in 2009, after her recovery from the second ACL tear, and while she could have played one more season for the Pilots, opted instead to turn pro. She was selected second overall by the Chicago Red Stars in the first ever Women's Professional Soccer draft, the second attempt at a women's professional league in America (only behind Amy Rodriguez, selected by the Boston Breakers).

She stayed in Chicago for two seasons, before the team was forced to cease operations in WPS. She landed with the Philadelphia Independence, before being traded to magicJack, a team located in Florida, during the 2011 season.

---

10   Ibid.

Rapinoe's first real taste of fame came in the 2011 World Cup, thanks to her role in That Goal—Abby Wambach's goal in extra time (the 122nd minute of the match, to be precise) to send the quarterfinal against Brazil to penalty kicks. Rapinoe's assist on the goal was sent in with her left foot, not her dominant one, not one that she thought she had enough power in to put the cross in the right place.

Except in this match, she did.

"I took one touch to push the ball ahead and looked up quickly toward Brazil's goal," Rapinoe wrote of her memory of how the assist went down a few years later, in 2014. "I saw a blur of four yellow jerseys and a green one (not my teammate—their goalkeeper). At that moment, I had to pass the ball to an invisible teammate. I knew that somewhere outside my peripheral vision, Abby Wambach was sprinting furiously into the box. I didn't know where she was. But I knew where she would be."[11]

The goal became an instant classic, and completely swung the momentum of the match—the United States went on to defeat Brazil via penalties, and faced Japan in the 2011 World Cup final.

America and the rest of the world also got their first real taste of Rapinoe's ability to celebrate a goal at full force. She sprinted to Wambach, leaping onto her and latching on for dear life. The photos from

---

11   Rapinoe, Megan. "The Cross," *The Players' Tribune*, December 16, 2014. www.theplayerstribune.com/en-us/articles/the-cross

that game show Rapinoe clinging to
hands wrapped so tightly around Wam
Rapinoe almost looks like she's tryin'
own teammate, not celebrate a goal. ⌐
Rapinoe being Rapinoe, and plenty of other teammates
over the years would experience that same leap after she
provided an assist.

Rapinoe reflected on how that tournament proved to
be a key turning point for the US national team, a full
two World Cup cycles later. If the 1996 Olympic Games
had led to the breakthrough moment of the 1999 World
Cup, Rapinoe's generation of the game forced the sport
back into national consciousness via their own World
Cup journey over the last decade.

Before the team left for the 2011 World Cup, they
played their final tune-up match in New Jersey, at Red
Bull Arena. The stadium is soccer-specific, and now the
US women's national team regularly fills every available
seat. But in May 2011, as the team struggled to find a
win against regional rivals Mexico, the stadium wasn't
even a quarter full. Rapinoe remembered the number as
around 7,000—it was actually only 5,852.

Heading to Germany for the tournament helped—
but the resurgence of the USWNT doesn't happen
without their performance at the 2011 World Cup, and
specifically, another World Cup win against Brazil. Even
without lifting the trophy in the final, Rapinoe and this
edition of the national team came back to America and
arrived as heroes.

"We didn't even win," Rapinoe wrote, "but it felt like a '99 moment for a new generation."[12]

Even as Rapinoe felt everything was changing, there were larger issues than could be overcome with the professional league, thanks in large part to the owner of magicJack. By early 2012, the league shuttered. Rapinoe and a few teammates, including goalkeeper Hope Solo and forward Alex Morgan, played a few matches for Seattle Sounders Women as part of a semi-pro league as a stopgap, especially with the 2012 Olympics coming up.

Before the Summer Games in London, Rapinoe came out publicly via an interview with *Out Magazine*, just a low-key confirmation without much fanfare. That decision would have long-lasting repercussions for her entire career, both on and off the field, but at the time it was just a simple affirmation of who she is as a person.

By 2013, Rapinoe signed a contract with French professional team Olympique Lyonnais even as a new women's professional league, the National Women's Soccer League, was taking shape. The money was much better in France, especially for someone like Rapinoe (she earned about $14,000 a month for her six-month contract), but

12   Rapinoe, Megan. "You Can't Get Rid of Your Girl That Easily," *The Players' Tribune*, June 23, 2019. www.theplayerstribune.com /en-us/articles/megan-rapinoe-united-states-world-cup-youre-not -gonna-get-rid-of-your-girl-that-easily

THE JOURNEY WILL SHAPE YOU • 13

there were other factors in looking abroad at this point in her career: getting a feel for the European approach to the game, perhaps adding some new dimensions to her skills.

Of course, there was also the simple fact that she was a professional player, who was paid to do so in France. "But really, who wouldn't do what I'm getting the chance to do if they had the chance?" she asked of the *New York Times* writer Sam Borden when he went out to visit her in Lyon.[13]

After the stint in Lyon, Rapinoe returned to the States for her NWSL debut, with Seattle Reign FC. She has been with the club since the first year of the league, and was a key part of their success in finishing first place in the regular season in both 2014 and 2015—even as the Reign would eventually fall in back-to-back championships against FC Kansas City.

At the 2015 World Cup in Canada, Rapinoe didn't have the outsized impact that she eventually would in 2019. She tallied two goals in the United States' first group-stage game against Australia, but after the round of 16, accumulated enough yellow cards to have to serve a one-match suspension. Carli Lloyd was the star of the final in 2015, scoring three goals—including a half-field stunner—to help bring a World Cup trophy back to America for the first time since 1999.

---

13 Borden, Sam. "A US Soccer Star's Declaration of Independence," The *New York Times*, April 10, 2013. www.nytimes.com/2013/04/11 /sports/soccer/megan-rapinoe-does-it-her-way-in-us-and-in-france .html

In December 2015, before a game that was scheduled for Hawaii as part of the post–2015 World Cup victory tour, Rapinoe ended up tearing her anterior cruciate ligament in her right knee. The timing couldn't have been worse when it came to the 2016 Olympics, and while Rapinoe did ultimately make that roster, she was not at full strength by any stretch of the imagination.

What came next was a time of transformation for Rapinoe—the ACL injury, her decision to kneel during the national anthem in 2016, meeting her girlfriend for the first time—her life changed drastically between the 2015 and 2019 World Cups.

"The last couple years have been interesting and fun and challenging," Rapinoe said before the 2019 World Cup. "I feel like I went through this one-year period, not even one year, right after I did my knee (in Hawaii), right then until October of the next year. Wasn't really playing that well, I knelt in support with Colin Kaepernick, I met Sue (Bird), and it was just a convergence of all these things that I'm actually so thankful for."[14]

Rapinoe said all of those things happening within the same year, as well as the loss in the Olympics, forced her to realize that she must make changes in her life.

---

14 "23 Stories: Megan Rapinoe," US Soccer. June 3, 2019. www .ussoccer.com/stories/2019/06/23-stories-megan-rapinoe

"Just as a person, you kind of go through those different seasons in life, but as an athlete who's getting a little bit older, you reach this time where you either get old really fast or you change and you have like, your second career. So I feel like it all happened right at that moment, and this is my second career."[15]

Rapinoe didn't prove to be a major factor in 2015 for the United States, but in 2019, she owned the World Cup tournament. She scored a goal in the team's opening group stage win over Thailand, a 13–0 romp. But she shined in the knock-out stages.

She converted two penalty kicks against Spain in the round of 16 to advance the US, then scored another pair in the quarterfinal against France. And while she sat out the semifinal against England thanks to a hamstring injury, her return for the final proved just as important, as she scored the game-winning goal against the Netherlands. By the end of the tournament, she'd scored six goals, been named Player of the Match three times, and won the tournament's Golden Ball for most goals scored as well as the Golden Boot for best player of the World Cup. The awards wouldn't stop in France, either.

Yet for all the attention and acclaim she earned on the field, Rapinoe would find a new level of fame off the field in 2019—thanks to a public feud with the President of the United States of America in the middle of the World Cup itself. Rapinoe was always willing to speak her mind, not just after her decision to kneel during the anthem,

15   Ibid.

but as part of the team's fight for equal pay against their own federation; but the mix of sports and politics on the biggest stage gave her the largest platform of her career.

And as she's shown time and time again, she's not afraid to use it.

Perhaps Rapinoe would have gotten there on her own, but that fundamental lesson from her own childhood, to put others before herself, ultimately carried through into her actions as an adult. Not everyone grows up to be a famous soccer player, obviously, but even as her own path defined her worldview and eventually her activism, she was not shaped only by soccer. Her family, her teammates, and her career all played a role in helping her understand what was most important, even when her own actions resulted in personal risks, especially to her career. Rapinoe grew as a player and as a human over the course of three and a half decades, but never let go of the most basic value to stand up for others.

And beyond Rapinoe's journey from childhood, there's also a key takeaway from her experience growing up and watching the US national team win in 1999, then her own role with the team at the 2011 World Cup (and all the subsequent ones). For both editions of the 1999 and 2015 and 2019 World Cup–winning squads, there was always something that came before to set the stage— the 1996 Olympics, the 2011 World Cup. Breakthroughs are only when others acknowledge the hard work it takes to publicly succeed, but often that hard work is done in front of smaller crowds, or no one at all.

At one point, Rapinoe thought no one was watching, that women's soccer wasn't really a thing that could grasp the attention span of the country again. Instead, she and her team and the sport itself captured plenty of eyeballs, but also an entire new generation of fans who suddenly found themselves dreaming—as Rapinoe had once before—of something they previously never dreamed possible.

CHAPTER TWO

Be authentic to who you are, even when it's tough

"It wasn't easy for me. But it shouldn't be."

MEGAN RAPINOE WASN'T BORN AN activist, there was no magical process that happened in Northern California that somehow created a loud, progressive, queer force for speaking up and using her platform. She was raised to stand up for herself and her family and other people, but that didn't necessarily translate into the Megan Rapinoe of 2020. It was just one piece.

"It wasn't like she was a social activist back in college," Stephanie Cox—a teammate in college, in Seattle, and the national team—told the *Guardian* in 2017. "She was just trying to figure out who she was.

She's definitely grown into that. It hasn't always been the case."[16]

Even as her upbringing in Redding shaped her values, her relationship with her hometown has changed over the course of her career, thanks in large part to Rapinoe's willingness to step into matters of politics. She dealt with this change within her own family, as well.

Her father, Jim, declared on the record to the local paper that he voted for Donald Trump in 2016. And even as Redding was proud of Rapinoe's success on the field, there was a clear tension between the residents back home and the local star the town produced.

Jim Rapinoe wasn't the only one in Redding voting for Trump after all; about 64 percent of Redding voted the same way, compared to about 28 percent voting for Hillary Clinton. There's also another factor in Redding, the presence of Bethel Church, a nondenominational megachurch that has opposed restrictions against conversion therapy, and whose faith leaders have been vocal supporters of Trump.

Tony Roberts, a resident of Redding, summed up the city's approach to Rapinoe as this, "We're proud our small town girl did great but keep your mouth shut. I respect your opinion. Just don't put it in my face."[17]

---

16   Pentz, Matt. "Megan Rapinoe: 'God forbid you be a gay woman and a person of color in the US,'" *The Guardian*, March 25, 2017. www.theguardian.com/football/2017/mar/25/megan-rapinoe-gay -woman-person-color-us
17   Almond, Elliott. "Women's World Cup: Hometown star stirs mixed feelings in California's Trump country," *The Mercury News*, July 6, 2019. www.mercurynews.com/2019/07/06/womens-world-cup -hometown-star-out-of-step-in-californias-trump-country/

Jim Rapinoe told the local paper in that same interview that he was proud of what his daughter stood for as an activist. "She's got her stances, and she is willing to fight for them and she is willing to sacrifice it all. When she did the kneeling thing, that could have been the end of her career." He also pointed to his own military service, and his father's before him. "That's what we go for, the right to be able to protest. She protests peacefully. She doesn't go out there and try to burn buildings down."[18]

Rapinoe was absolutely aware of this tension—and in fact set it aside when she raised donations after wildfires affected Redding in 2018. She understood the city, the larger community as a whole, was conservative and voted for Proposition 8 and Donald Trump.

"I think my views, my political stances, are probably very different from a lot of people. I think the kneeling was a big thing. Even just stories of people coming in and saying stuff to my mom in the restaurant or saying stuff to my family members, obviously, I think it was a very hot button issue," she told espnW in 2018 in a story from Graham Hays on her fundraising efforts for the Carr fires.[19]

Rapinoe grew beyond her hometown when it came to politics, but she did say their support has never wavered even as they don't see eye to eye on all things. When she

18 Ibid.
19 Hays, Graham. "Megan Rapinoe launches fire relief fund for Redding hometown," *ESPN*, August 26, 2018. www.espn.com/espnw /sports/story/_/id/24486574/us-soccer-star-megan-rapinoe-launches -fire-relief-fund-redding-hometown

goes back home, she receives plenty of love and support. That doesn't mean it's unanimous.

Rapinoe received strong reactions on her fundraiser, told directly by people that because of her politics, she wasn't going to get donations on behalf of Redding. She didn't allow the pushback to deter her from raising money, as she viewed her personal beliefs as an entirely separate thing from her efforts to help her hometown. And based on the way she was raised, Rapinoe felt the call of responsibility to help, to look out for others before she looked out for herself.

Even as the relationship between her and Redding grew more complicated, Rapinoe was never about to forget where she was from, or how it shaped her life. Even if her hometown's values didn't exactly line up with her own, it didn't erase all the lessons Redding taught her.

"I feel like Redding is kind of this underdog, hard-working, blue-collar, is-what-it-is kind of town, and I try to take that with me," Rapinoe said. "I never want to just say, 'Oh, I'm from California.' I'm not from California; I'm from Redding. For me, that means something."[20]

At the same time, leaving Redding opened up her world. She understood the demographics of the city for what they were, but she also didn't even have the vocabulary to name her own sexuality before she went to college at the University of Portland.

"Redding, California, where I grew up, is quite homogeneous racially, and sexuality-wise, and politically," she

20 Ibid.

said in 2019.[21] "It was all kind of the same thing. I didn't have a repressive or oppressive childhood by any means, it was just 'gay' was never spoken."

That move north to Portland, only about a seven-hour drive by I-5, meant a new world.

"Once I got to college and these things started to be named and there were other gay people, I was sort of forced to think for myself," Rapinoe said. "It was, 'Oh, well, this is a thing, and that is a thing, and this is why people are Democrats, and this is what liberal means, you know?' It's like, I'd known things before, but they'd never been named."[22]

She also found a new world via US Soccer. Even as the start of her career was derailed by the two ACL tears, she traveled to Thailand as part of the Under-19 FIFA Women's World Cup in 2004. She trained at the same camps as her national team idols, like Kristine Lilly. That environment, along with the one at University of Portland, helped her find people that could teach her in new ways, with different backgrounds and viewpoints.

21   Marchese, David. "Megan Rapinoe is in celebration mode. And she's got some things to say." The *New York Times Magazine*, July 29, 2019. www.nytimes.com/interactive/2019/07/29/magazine /megan-rapinoe-sports-politics.html
22   Ibid.

That environment, as well as her friendships on the team, also meant that she felt safe and supported coming out before the 2012 Olympics.

"I think the climate that we set on the team of acceptance and love is really amazing. We're not all the very best of friends, but I think at the very basic level, we love and respect each other. And I've definitely felt that, before I came out and quite a lot after I came out."[23]

That respect amongst the team, even as individual goals had to be met, can be translated to the dynamics of being an activist. The team holds each person accountable, even as it supports them. The team supports learning on the fly, without expecting perfection on the training field, as long as it's executed on game day and gets results. Collective leadership and collective effort is key, even as players like captains and veterans step forward to take greater weight on their shoulders. Even if players are on the bench, they still play an important role.

Ultimately, the locker room sets the tone. And Rapinoe has been a key piece of driving that for the past couple of years.

Head coach Jill Ellis named Megan Rapinoe a co-captain of the US national team before the team set out for World Cup qualifying in 2019, alongside fellow veterans Alex Morgan and Carli Lloyd.

23 "Megan Rapinoe Accepts LGBT Award | LA LGBT Center," *YouTube*, uploaded by Los Angeles LGBT Center, November 12, 2012. https://youtu.be/tSgcLb8AeQ8

"I think that what I've seen in Pinoe in meetings and on the pitch is just a willingness to extend herself to her teammates," Ellis said in an interview during the 2018 qualifiers with ESPN.[24] "Whether it's a comment when we're watching film or out on the field going over to players, really extending herself to help them in decision-making. What I saw in there was a player that could have an influence—off the field, great personality, fun to be around but also has an intensity about her."

By the time she finally earned the right to the captain's armband, it was a full twelve years after her first call-up in 2006, essentially a decade since she actually joined the team in a more dedicated capacity after her ACL tears. And while her position was never fully guaranteed during that decade-plus, a span which included yet another ACL tear plus other injuries, the player that emerged from the other side had something to give as a leader.

"She is just instantly credible in terms of the experiences she's been through and her résumé to this point," said Ellis.[25]

By the time the World Cup rolled around, Rapinoe started joking that she felt like the "old grandma" of the team, but that being a part of the journeys of the younger players was something she took a lot of personal joy in.

24 Hays, Graham. "From boos to captain's armband, Megan Rapinoe is better than ever," *ESPN*, October 9, 2018. www.espn.com /espnw/sports/story/_/id/24942605/from-boos-captain-armband -megan-rapinoe-better-ever-us-women-soccer-team
25 Ibid.

"They're such a huge part of this team, to see them grow within that and be so excited for their first World Cup, it's just the best," she said.[26]

At the same time, Rapinoe could only be a leader on the team because she fully embraced her own identity and her own journey, and encouraged every single other player to do the exact same thing.

Even when the environment was challenging, the trainings were repetitive, it was the people within this small world that meant the difference between success and failure. "The people in it make it interesting and challenging and fun, help you grow and keep you sane," she said.

Without her personal growth through her third torn ACL, kneeling, meeting Bird, she was taking that second career and bringing something new to her role as captain, treating it as an extension of her approach to life—one driven by her identity and values. Rapinoe used those challenges to figure out who she was as a person—the tests revealed what she valued most. She then brought that energy to the team.

Rapinoe's energy wasn't just a natural byproduct of her life experiences; she was intentional in turning those experiences into something that would be productive for others and for the environment of the national team. Rapinoe actively chose to be intentional with how her identity impacts others.

---

26 "23 Stories: Megan Rapinoe," US Soccer. June 3, 2019. www .ussoccer.com/stories/2019/06/23-stories-megan-rapinoe

For Rapinoe, being intentional feels lighter, not like work. Being herself, not the expectations of who she should be as a player or a leader or a human, is easier. That lightness is contagious. The intentionality is shared—everyone is encouraged to be themselves; rather than buying into a competitive mentality against others, there's only pressure to be yourself. In Rapinoe's mind, that's not a pressure at all, that's a gift.

At the same time she was bringing her new self to the table, she also needed to find new ways to balance her soccer career and everything off the field.

"My capacity is constantly being expanded," she said.[27] At that moment when you are totally overwhelmed and can't do anymore, it's really cool to lean into that and always demand more of yourself and see where you can do more, be more and challenge yourself in those ways."

That she had been named captain after the kneeling incident and resulting response from US Soccer was interesting enough. The World Cup thrust Rapinoe into a very different level of fame than Carli Lloyd experienced in 2015.

---

27   Parker, Maggie. "How Soccer Star Megan Rapinoe Remains Hopeful: 'Don't F*** with Us,'" *Parade Magazine*, October 22, 2019. parade.com/940125/maggie_parker/us-womens-soccer-player -megan-rapinoe-self-care-women-empowerment/

Even adjusting to the new reality of her life was taking some work.

"A lot of it is unknown, and you have to figure it out as it comes, but I think something that's been easier for me is that I got famous for all the things I am anyway," she said. "It's not like I said something crazy—" she paused "—I mean, not more than normal. I've been saying all these things for all this time, it's just at an elevated level."[28]

Of course, she was also wholeheartedly embracing the fact that more people were listening than ever, not just to her, but to the US national team as a whole, particularly on the issue of equal pay.

"It puts us in a better position," she said. "And we're like, 'Yeah! We've been fucking telling you this forever!'"[29]

There is a difference between being a good teammate and a good ally, but the foundation is not too far off: the concept that you must make the fight your own, that there is a force larger than yourself. The US women's national team took steps of their own to turn the team into something more political than just the representation of America on the international stage—they used the team and its power to fight for equal pay and equal respect.

---

28 Linehan, Meg. "'I got famous for all the things I am anyway': Megan Rapinoe on transforming from activist to icon," *The Athletic*, August 21, 2019. theathletic.com/1152922/
29 Ibid.

Rapinoe came to terms with what being an ally meant firsthand in 2016. She learned it was upon herself to make sure she was educated in the issues she wanted to discuss, she made sure she didn't take credit for the work that was previously accomplished, and she constantly reframed her own role within the context of the power and privilege that she possessed.

"It wasn't easy for me, but it shouldn't be," Rapinoe said in 2019.[30] "Whenever you're trying to be an ally, and it's super easy and comfortable for you, you're not an ally." Rapinoe learned these lessons after following in the footsteps of Colin Kaepernick, as well as advocating for racial justice alongside queer rights. Again, the tests she faced in the latter part of her career proved instrumental in figuring out what she valued, as well as the work ahead for society as a whole.

"I think that was a really good lesson for me: This is what it's going to take for things to change, norms to change, conventions to change, to try to break down white supremacy and break down racial bias," Rapinoe said. "It's going to take it being hard. For everyone."[31]

While these larger issues seemed daunting and remained unsolved, Rapinoe found a new strength and clearer focus on her role and priorities. Instead of deciding that her values and her career as an athlete

---

30 Bushnell, Henry. "Megan Rapinoe is a 'walking protest,'" *Yahoo! Sports*, May 13, 2019. sports.yahoo.com/megan-rapinoe-is-a-walking -protest-162416461.html
31 Ibid.

were incompatible, and that she would need to choose one over the other, Rapinoe threaded a line that served both. Playing for the national team and in the NWSL meant her voice carried a little louder—and while it also meant that some shouted back, or cut her off entirely— she pushed at the limits of what was permissible. While Rapinoe couldn't always say everything she might want to say, she continued to say most of it. She stayed true to herself. She stayed authentic to her values. And ultimately, she found out what was most important to her when that seemed the hardest to do because of the backlash.

CHAPTER THREE
Let your identity guide you

"Being gay has shaped my life's view."

THE MONTH BEFORE THE 2012 Olympic Games in London, Megan Rapinoe came out via an interview with *Out Magazine*.[32] There was nothing deeply personal in the interview or revelatory about her approach to life—and in a small, amusing detail, the story is actually filed to the travel section and tagged to London, thanks to the story's hook of the Olympic Games—just a simple confirmation that she was gay, and had been dating someone for three years.

"I feel everyone is really craving (for) people to come out," she told *Out.* "People want—they need—to see

---

32   Portwood, Jerry. "Fever Pitch," *Out Magazine*, July 2, 2012. www .out.com/travel-nightlife/london/2012/07/02/fever-pitch

that there are people like me playing soccer for the good ol' US of A."

The quote was an early indication that Rapinoe knew the power of her platform already. Not just the platform of a professional athlete, but the platform that comes thanks to playing on the US national team and representing the country at events like the Olympics or the World Cup.

Back in 2012, the reach of Rapinoe's platform was not nearly as wide—yes, there was additional coverage of major international tournaments; yes, there was coverage of the US national team, but interest in the players, their performance, their personal stories, was not exactly sustained by mainstream culture or sports fans across the entirety of a four-year cycle between World Cups. As much as Rapinoe's performance in 2011 helped her gain recognition, her sphere of influence was considerably smaller at the start of the decade.

Still, the choice to come out cannot be overlooked, even if it seems an obvious one in hindsight. Other female athletes previously walked this road before across multiple sports, but the situation on the men's professional sports side was—and remains—remarkably different. Robbie Rogers, an American soccer player then playing professionally in England, came out in 2013 at the same time he announced he was retiring (though a few months later, he returned to the game, signing with the Los Angeles Galaxy of MLS). Shortly after, Jason Collins came out while still an active player in the NBA.

The pressures for LGBT athletes, no matter the gender, are not very different: Will the decision to come out lose them sponsorships and endorsements? Will a player's identity be reduced to one defining characteristic, will there be homophobic harassment on the field or from the stands or through social media, will it cause problems with teammates or coaches or management who might not want to deal with the attention?

Every case is different. But visibility has been a key, historically, for the gay rights movement in opposing homophobia.

For Rapinoe, there was an awareness of not just queer history and the challenges faced by professional athletes in coming out. But there were also the specifics of the history of the US women's national team itself, and the image of the team curated by the federation and its sponsors, internally and externally, of what type of women played for the team.

Rapinoe knew she was pushing some boundaries. US Soccer presented the 1999 edition of the team to America as the friendly girls next door. The players featured lovely smiles and ponytails, and while they won a World Cup, they weren't threatening. They were charming, demographically almost entirely white, and extremely heteronormative. That image didn't tell the entire story of the team—there were varying personalities, they were dominating in their play, they were tough and played through injuries and illnesses—but that image is the one that helped define the nature of the team for years.

By 2012, the national team did look different, but the idea that the team—as much as they were known for playing soccer—also served as role models for the next generation of young girls was still hard to escape. It's a concept that still has its sway over the team even now, with pushback over the team's celebrations, cursing, if it's arrogance or confidence, a seemingly endless debate over the respectability of this team.

Adding Rapinoe's open queerness to the mix in 2012 helped push the conversation along, but it also helped open up the conversation of what sort of role models the team had to be, and for whom.

She also didn't make the decision alone—it took encouragement from her friend and teammate Lori Lindsey, and then support from her agent, her family, and other friends.

Rapinoe told the story of how the process actually started in November of 2012, and Lindsey's direct role in her decision-making. Their conversation happened on the flight back from the 2011 World Cup, in the immediate aftermath of both the highest high via the win over Brazil in the quarterfinal and a 3–1 victory over France in the semi, and the lowest low as the US lost via penalty kicks to Japan in the final. Rapinoe called the loss devastating, so the mood on the flight was a bit heavier than usual, even as the team tried to keep it light.

As Rapinoe recalled, she was sitting across from Lindsey on the plane, and Lindsey brought up the subject of coming out unprompted, and her tone was serious.

There was no justification, just the simple statement that it was past time for Rapinoe to formally come out.

"This is from the horse's mouth," Rapinoe said, "[Lindsey] looks me dead in the eye, she goes, 'I'm not fucking around. Turn around, talk to Dan right now.'"[33]

The Dan in question was Rapinoe's agent, Dan Levy. And Rapinoe did as she was told, moving from one conversation to the next, and telling Levy that she wanted to come out—more than that, that she needed to. Levy, for his part, didn't try to talk her out of it, but simply got to work.

"I think that moment was a turning point for me of the question in my head, of should I come out, is it the right time to—why would I ever not come out?" Rapinoe said a year later. "Why would I never not take this stand, and say this is who I am? And I'm very proud of that."[34]

Rapinoe called Lindsey the "spark and the fire" she needed to start the process. Lindsey herself was only a few months behind Rapinoe in coming out, which she did through an interview with *Autostraddle*, an independent queer news and culture site. She shared it via her own Twitter account, joking, "You're going to need to sit down for this one! It's going to come as a real shock…"[35]

33 "Megan Rapinoe Accepts LGBT Award | LA LGBT Center," *YouTube*, uploaded by Los Angeles LGBT Center, November 12, 2012. https://youtu.be/tSgcLb8AeQ8
34 Ibid.
35 @LoriLindsey6, Twitter, September 5, 2012. twitter.com /LoriLindsey6/status/243435477590499328

In that interview, Lindsey joked that she was mad Rapinoe actually beat her to coming out, even though it was originally her idea. "I think Megan is a wonderful role model for anybody—for straights, gays, everybody. So more power to her. I'm just proud that I can follow in her footsteps," she said, laughing. "I'm just kidding."[36]

Even as fellow players like Lindsey and Abby Wambach came out, then eventually retired from their professional soccer careers, Rapinoe was key in opening that door to other players as a viable option. By 2019, she certainly wasn't the only out player on the US national team. There were multiple forms of expression of queerness and different personalities on the team, providing a better range of humanity—and showing there's no one correct way to be a queer female athlete on the world's stage.

"This means so much to thousands of people," *SBNation*'s Kim McCauley wrote right after the 2019 World Cup final, spurred on by Kelley O'Hara's celebration after the win, simply finding her partner in the stands and giving her a kiss without any comment or formal coming out.

"'Pride' is such an apt word for LGBT+ celebrations because it's what so many of us lacked for huge chunks of our lives," she wrote. "It's important for everyone, of any sexual orientation or gender identity, to feel some pride in who they are. That's often a lot harder for queer

36   Lora. "Lori Lindsey, USWNT Dark Horse: The Autostraddle Coming Out Interview," *Autostraddle*, September 5, 2012. www .autostraddle.com/lori-lindsey-144999/

people than it is for cisgender, heterosexual people. And seeing openly queer athletes become the best in the world at something like soccer, that's so visible and so important to most of the world, helps a lot of people find some pride in themselves on days when it's hard to muster any at all."[37]

McCauley also noted that Rapinoe's approach to her own identity isn't for everyone, especially those who are early in their journeys, who are closeted or questioning. She is fully committed at all times, but that level might not be attainable from day one for most people. And to be fair, Rapinoe took years of her career to get to her current level of comfort when it comes to her sexuality and identity. People looking for community or ties to queer people and spaces might admire Rapinoe, but it's not the only path available.

Still, Rapinoe's confidence paved the way for other teammates to follow in her footsteps. These conversations wouldn't have been successful without that confidence, and her candidness about her identity. She's always had the confidence part down, but she didn't always have the identity part figured out. Remarkably, that took her heading to college to finally have the pieces click into place.

"I didn't know that I was gay, frankly, until I was in college," she told the *New York Times Magazine*. "Until then I was like, 'Everything feels weird.' I think being

---

37   McCauley, Kim. "Why the USWNT's open queerness matters," *SB Nation*, July 7, 2019. www.sbnation.com/soccer/2019/7/7/20685477/why-the-uswnts-open-queerness-matters

gay, it's like you're not going to ever be normal, so you don't have rules, and if you don't have to follow any rules, all bets are off. A lot of my confidence comes from that, from not feeling societal pressure to be anything other than what I want to be. My natural disposition is to have confidence, but certainly, figuring out that I was gay, I was like, 'Oh, God!' Looking back, it's embarrassing because, duh."[38]

In the four years after graduating the University of Portland and starting her professional career during the Women's Professional Soccer era, no reporters ever asked. So she took matters into her own hands to go on the record, to state her identity publicly.

There was real power in this decision, and her visible queerness while representing the United States. But at this point in her career, she was still the same person who scored a goal in the 2011 World Cup and celebrated by picking up a field mic and belting Bruce Springsteen's "Born in the USA" directly into it. She was playing soccer "for the good ol' US of A." She was growing as a player on the field with every practice and every game, but this was the first real step in Rapinoe's awakening and journey off the field in pushing the limits of her platform.

38   Marchese, David. "Megan Rapinoe is in celebration mode. And she's got some things to say." The *New York Times Magazine*, July 29, 2019. www.nytimes.com/interactive/2019/07/29/magazine/megan-rapinoe-sports-politics.html

By the time post–World Cup 2019 rolled around, Rapinoe was calling herself a "a pink-haired, unapologetically flaming gay lesbian."[39] More importantly, she knew that her identity shaped her entire approach to her activism.

Her perspective had shifted because she was queer. While she personally did not think she had experienced much in the way of homophobia, she still knew she was not necessarily a "regular white girl" either.

Thanks to the hindsight of her own journey over the past fifteen years, Rapinoe understood how being gay also opened the doors to solidarity with other movements. And for Rapinoe, there's an inherently political element to being a female athlete. Even that designation of gender in front of the word athlete indicates that there is a distinction, an othering. Men's sports are simply sports. Women's sports remain women's sports. That marker provides a notable jumping-off point.

Women's sports fight for respect, investment, and coverage. Men's sports leagues, such as the National Football League, Major League Baseball, National Basketball Association, and others, have existed for decades. Women's soccer never had a similar luxury of time to grow a fanbase. Two previous leagues shuttered after three years each; the National Women's Soccer League looks to be on firmer footing, but still hasn't reached double digits in age. US Soccer began a women's senior

---

39   Ibid.

national team in 1985, after Title IX helped grow the game at the college level.

Women who play sports professionally are usually on the outside looking in, though there are some exceptions. Billie Jean King helped pave the way for equality in tennis, and athletes like Serena and Venus Williams benefitted. But Rapinoe's always been a part of a sport that's constantly being asked to justify its own existence. Worse still, there are still plenty of men on the Internet ready to comment with, "Get back in the kitchen" whenever they happen to come across a highlight from women's sports.

Mix society's reluctance to embrace women's sports with being queer, and Rapinoe's experienced that combination her entire career—but that combativeness encouraged her to speak up more.

"Part of it is just who I am, I am gay so there's that aspect, and I am a female athlete," she said in an interview with *Parade* after the 2019 World Cup. "So there is a lot of activism potential in there. I feel like female athletes are always on the forefront of anything activism because the intersectionality of us all just runs so deep— we're women of color, gay, we're women."[40]

In 2012 when she came out, Rapinoe wasn't talking about concepts like intersectionality—simply trying to live an authentic life. But over the course of her

---

40   Parker, Maggie. "How Soccer Star Megan Rapinoe Remains Hopeful: 'Don't F*** with Us,'" *Parade Magazine*, October 22, 2019. parade.com/940125/maggie_parker/us-womens-soccer-player-megan -rapinoe-self-care-women-empowerment/

career, as the political fortunes of the "good ol' US of A" changed from the Obama era of the White House through the 2016 election, there was a clear shift in both how Rapinoe approached her own identity and how it affected her worldview. She had always been willing to speak her mind, but her mind was now working through problems on a much larger scale.

It's not that these were new issues—they weren't. But as Rapinoe educated herself about gay rights, the more she realized how intertwined they were with other civil rights movements, and her lens through which she viewed the power dynamics of the world came into focus more clearly.

In 1983, American poet, essayist, and civil rights activist Audre Lorde wrote that there is no hierarchy of oppression. Lorde's identity encompassed both being Black and a lesbian—the Black community had its share of LGBTQ people, the LGBTQ community had its share of Black people.

"I cannot afford the luxury of fighting one form of oppression only," Lorde wrote. "I cannot afford to believe that freedom from intolerance is the right of only one particular group. And I cannot afford to choose between the fronts upon which I must battle these forms of discrimination, wherever they appear to destroy me. And when they appear to destroy me, it will not be long before they appear to destroy you."[41]

---

41 Lorde, Audre. "There is no hierarchy of oppressions," Council on Interracial Books for Children, 1983.

Thirty-six years later, Rapinoe would wear Audre Lorde's name on the back of her jersey—part of a special event from US Soccer as part of the SheBelieves Tournament (an invitational set of games that takes place yearly in the United States). With the tournament's name and mission statement designed around the concept of role models and encouraging young women, the federation took advantage of International Women's Day lining up with the 2019 tournament, and invited players to wear the names of women they found inspirational.

"Audre Lorde was unapologetically herself," Rapinoe told the US Soccer communications staff, providing the reasoning for her selection. "She so beautifully and powerfully expressed all parts of herself and her experiences at once. She was a woman, a lesbian, a feminist, a person of color, a civil right activist and a poet. She understood so clearly that change does not come from playing by the existing set of rules.

"I hope that wearing her name on the back of my jersey will encourage more people, myself included, to learn about her as a person, engage with her writing, and appreciate how influential one person can be," Rapinoe said.[42]

Rapinoe wasn't trying to wear her name to suggest that she wanted to reach that level of influence, just point

---

42 "WNT honors inspirational women with names on back of jerseys at SheBelieves Cup," US Soccer, March 2, 2019. www.ussoccer.com/stories/2019/03/wnt-honors-inspirational-women-with-names-on-back-of-jerseys-at-shebelieves-cup

at a thinker who had opened up her own eyes. Ultimately, Rapinoe always wanted to act more as a conduit to conversation, rather than serving as some sort of thought leader.

She's also still in the middle of her own education. As she said, she still wants to learn more about Audre Lorde and to engage with her writing, but her education goes beyond that. Intersectionality has been the center of this self-driven learning experience.

"The more I've been able to learn about gay rights and equal pay and gender equity and racial inequality, the more that it all intersects," Rapinoe told Matt Pentz in 2017. "You can't really pick it apart. It's all intertwined. God forbid you be a gay woman and a person of color in this country, because you'd be really fucked."[43]

Rapinoe said in August of 2019 that she became famous for all the things she was already saying. She wasn't joking, either. In that same interview from 2017 with Pentz, she was tying her identity to issues that mattered to her, and pointing at the conversations that still needed to be held.

Before she wore Lorde's name on the back of her jersey, she echoed the exact same argument Lorde was making in the 1980s: these fights are all intertwined. Rapinoe's awakening involved gay rights, but also equal

---

43   Pentz, Matt. "Megan Rapinoe: 'God forbid you be a gay woman and a person of color in the US,'" *The Guardian*, March 25, 2017. www.theguardian.com/football/2017/mar/25/megan-rapinoe-gay -woman-person-color-us

pay—and both were connected. She asked for conversations that addressed equality from a much larger perspective, and respect for everyone. Driving this need in a new light: the 2016 election and the "subsequent narrative that's coming from the White House right now."[44]

That's not to say that everything is deeply serious for Rapinoe either—there is also a fundamental joy to her personality and her worldview.

Following the 2015 World Cup win, Rapinoe went on ESPN's SportsCenter and was asked to describe herself in one word. With a white board in hand, Rapinoe revealed her answer with complete glee.

"GAAAAY," she wrote, complete with a smiley face at the end, shouting out her answer at the same time.[45]

Thanks to her embrace of both the politics and the playfulness of her queerness, Rapinoe presents a more complete and more human identity. She hasn't dropped the fun side either. In 2019, instead of waiting for the press tour back stateside, she had an audience to entertain during the World Cup itself.

In front of an absolutely jam-packed mixed zone at Parc des Princes in Paris, after scoring the two goals that helped advance the US national team through the quarterfinals over France, she was asked if there was anything special to having such a huge performance during

44   Ibid.
45   "Megan Rapinoe, describe yourself in one word." Vine, ESPN SportsCenter, July 9, 2015. vine.co/v/en36KuhuB0H/

Pride—a celebration Paris was also in the middle of at the same time as the World Cup.

"Go gays!" she said, clearly in a good mood after the game, and ready as ever to deliver some epic quotes.

"You can't win a championship without gays on your team, it's pretty much never been done before, ever," she said. "Science right there." (The quote would go on to inspire plenty of signs at the team's celebratory parade in New York City.)

Thanks to the increased scrutiny she was under at the World Cup—already having gone through news cycles involving how she celebrated scoring a goal against Thailand in the team's group stage opener, then plenty more about her refusal to go to the White House—for as much fun as she was having that night in Paris, there was still the understanding that there would be a negative reaction to literally anything she said.

"I don't really get energized by haters, or all that," she said in the mixed zone.

On the flip side, she acknowledged that there were sources of a more positive nature for her.

"I feel like there are so many more people that love me, so I'm like, 'Yay! People love me! This is great!' I'm a little more energized by that. I take more energy from that than trying to prove everyone wrong all the time— that's sort of draining to me," she said.

After all: "To be gay and fabulous during Pride Month at the World Cup is nice."

The moment in the mixed zone was more than just fun, or a source of laughter and some furious writing for everyone who wanted to capture a good quote. Because Rapinoe explicitly tied her queerness to her political identity, because she embraced the largest platform she ever held in her career, in the midst of the national team's campaign to repeat as World Cup champions and add a fourth star over their crest, the moment was heightened.

There was also power at doing this at a World Cup— an event that has not just shied away from the concept of Pride and celebrating it as it overlaps with the tournament, but FIFA, the governing body of international soccer, is almost entirely allergic to any sort of political elements creeping in whatsoever.

Of course, it's impossible to avoid or erase politics from a World Cup. Any international tournament means that players are representing their countries, which are political entities themselves. Sports, as with every facet of human existence, are inherently political.

From her awakening in college over the span of her time there in 2005 to 2008, to her coming out in 2012, followed by her own continued education in what it means to be gay and how it intersects with other marginalized identities, Rapinoe helped to redefine the reach of an out, queer, female athlete. She also—in part— redefined the image of the US national team, of American professional soccer players in general. She's shaped her platform and her goals in life through her identity. She found joy while doing it all.

Most importantly, her own identity helped her understand her world, and her role to play in it. While she embraced her identity wholeheartedly, Rapinoe knew that other members of the LGBTQ community were more at risk. She learned from other female athletes and looked at the world with an intersectional view.

Rapinoe's identity has guided her—especially as she leaned into becoming an ally and an activist—out of her own reality and understanding of her community. Her queerness gave her empathy and solidarity for others, helped her to be an ally for other marginalized groups. And in 2016, she was about to go through her greatest test as an ally yet.

CHAPTER FOUR

Your identity and your values must result in solidarity and allyship

"It's my responsibility to be an ally for other people."

AS MUCH AS RAPINOE HAS been asking for a conversation about larger issues in America over the past few years, she's also been issuing a call to action the entire time.

Rapinoe needs allies and in turn is ready to be an ally herself. She needs allies in the equal pay fight for the US national team and for herself as a queer person, but having such support does not come without reciprocal responsibility. In turn, she views herself as needing to step up for others, even if their life experiences fall outside what she knows directly.

She has taken that responsibility seriously, never more so than with her decision to kneel during the national anthem in the fall of 2016, showing her solidarity for NFL player Colin Kaepernick's protest.

"I am not going to stand up to show pride in a flag for a country that oppresses black people and people of color," Kaepernick told NFL Media in an interview that took place after he sat during the anthem following a 49ers preseason game on August 26, 2016.[46] By the 49ers' next game on September 1, he changed the mechanism of his protest to kneeling during the anthem after a conversation with a former Green Beret, Nate Boyer.

Boyer explained to him that sitting might read as disrespectful to veterans, and his message might get lost in the response. "It's hard for a lot of people to get past the gesture because of when it's happening," Boyer told the *Los Angeles Times*. "It's during the anthem, and that's a sacred time for a lot of people."[47]

"To me, this is bigger than football and it would be selfish on my part to look the other way," Kaepernick said. There are bodies in the street and people getting paid leave and getting away with murder."[48]

---

46 "Colin Kaepernick explains why he sat during national anthem," NFL.com, August 27, 2016. www.nfl.com/news/colin-kaepernick-explains-why-he-sat-during-national-anthem-0ap3000000691077
47 Farmer, Sam. "Must Reads: The ex-Green Beret who inspired Colin Kaepernick to kneel instead of sit during the anthem would like to clear a few things up," *The Los Angeles Times*, September 17, 2018. latimes.com/sports/nfl/la-sp-kaepernick-kneel-boyer-20180916-story.html
48 "Colin Kaepernick explains why he sat during national anthem," NFL.com, August 27, 2016. www.nfl.com/news/colin-kaepernick-explains-why-he-sat-during-national-anthem-0ap3000000691077

The 49ers did issue a statement of support following Kaepernick's initial protest, stating that the team respected the right to freedom of expression, and thus respected Kaepernick's right to choose how he saw fit to participate in any sort of traditions surrounding the national anthem.

By September 1, Kaepernick's teammate Eric Reid joined him by kneeling during the anthem. Other NFL players followed suit. But even from the first time he refused to stand for the anthem, Kaepernick was ready to accept whatever the fall-out was—even if it meant serious setbacks for his NFL career or personal sponsorships.

"I am not looking for approval. I have to stand up for people that are oppressed," he said in that same interview with NFL Media. "If they take football away, my endorsements from me, I know that I stood up for what is right."[49]

On September 4, 2016, Megan Rapinoe followed Kaepernick's lead. She didn't actually kneel during the anthem at a US national team game first. Her first protest actually occurred during a Seattle Reign FC match against the Chicago Red Stars, in Chicago. Rapinoe didn't even start the match, but knelt on the sideline, a few steps away from the rest of the substitutes. That distance might have been as simple as edging forward to be able to kneel on the grass of the pitch, but it made a striking image—alone, head unbowed.

---

49   Ibid.

Rapinoe was the first player from another sport to join Kaepernick, as well as the first white athlete to do so. More would follow.

"It was very intentional," Rapinoe told John Halloran, a Chicago-based women's soccer writer, after the game. "It was a little nod to Kaepernick and everything that he's standing for right now. I think it's actually pretty disgusting the way he was treated and the way that a lot of the media has covered it and made it about something that it absolutely isn't."[50]

Rapinoe, on message as always, stated her desire for a better dialogue about the actual issues at hand. She asked for more thoughtful conversations about race in America, that went both ways. She wasn't attempting to close herself off or put herself beyond question, but rather to simply highlight the issue for further discussion.

But from the jump, Rapinoe tied her queerness to her decision to protest during the national anthem, and her decision to be an ally to Colin Kaepernick and people of color.

"Being a gay American, I know what it means to look at the flag and not have it protect all of your liberties," she said after the conclusion of the Reign–Red Stars match. "It was something small that I could do and something that I plan to keep doing in the future and

50   Halloran, John. "Megan Rapinoe Kneels For Anthem at NWSL Match," *American Soccer Now*, September 4, 2016. americansoccernow.com/articles/megan-rapinoe-kneels-for-anthem -at-nwsl-match

hopefully spark some meaningful conversation around it. It's important to have white people stand in support of people of color on this. We don't need to be the leading voice, of course, but standing in support of them is something that's really powerful."[51]

Ultimately, she didn't view it as a large sacrifice either—just a gesture of support. Later that night, she tweeted, "It's the least I can do. Keep the conversation going."[52]

★ ★ ★

As ill-equipped as the NFL was to have a meaningful conversation about the nature of protest, let alone the actual statement Kaepernick was trying to make about police brutality, women's soccer was even less prepared.

Three days after Rapinoe knelt in Chicago, the Reign were scheduled for another regular-season match against the Washington Spirit on the road, this time in Boyds, Maryland. Rapinoe went on the record that she intended to continue kneeling during the national anthem at NWSL games. In Maryland, she didn't even get the chance.

Thanks to a decision made by the Washington Spirit's owner at the time, Bill Lynch, both the Spirit and the Reign—including Rapinoe—were intentionally

---

51 Ibid.
52 @mPinoe, Twitter, September 4, 2016. twitter.com/mPinoe/status /772611178652504064

kept in the locker rooms as the team played the national anthem ahead of schedule, much to the surprise of fans, the players, even the NWSL commissioner who was attending the match in person.

The team released a statement to explain the "owner-ship decision" to play the anthem early in order to avoid Rapinoe's protest, citing in one paragraph Lynch's own military service and a history of the national anthem being played before sporting events.

And while Lynch and the ownership of the team admitted in their own statement that the move would be viewed as "extraordinary" (generally a code word for knowing that something won't go over well), they also stated that it was their best option to "avoid taking focus away from the game on such an important night for our franchise."

While the statement was released by the team itself, it was simply an explanation of Lynch's thought pro-cess—and his justification for playing the anthem early fell apart the longer the statement got. Lynch acknowl-edged Rapinoe's right to free speech, but also called her planned protest a "hijacking of our organization's event to draw attention to what is ultimately a personal—albeit worthy—cause."[53]

But for Lynch, even allowing Rapinoe her right to free speech and protest essentially meant that the Washington Spirit were allowing the national anthem to be "hijacked,"

53 "Statement Regarding Washington Spirit Ownership Decision to Play the National Anthem Ahead of Schedule Tonight," via Tweet, @JeffKassouf, September 7, 2016. twitter.com/JeffKassouf /status/773669540471443456

an act he viewed as disrespectful. Lynch also pointed to the fact that athletes have a platform and an ability to have a deeper conversation about an issue. But he unilaterally decided that Rapinoe's kneeling during the anthem was not a conversation. He wanted her to articulate this via television interviews, not before one of his team's games—and certainly not while, in his mind, insulting the military or fans of the Washington Spirit.

History has not proven any of Lynch's argument correct, for what it's worth—the game ultimately mattered very little for the Spirit, but is remembered for the team's decision regarding the anthem.

But needless to say, Rapinoe was not impressed by the decision.

"To be honest I didn't hear (the anthem) and I wasn't exactly sure why it wasn't played but fucking unbelievable," Rapinoe said after the match. "Saddened by it. I think that it's pretty clear what the message is that I'm trying to bring to light when I knelt in Chicago and what I've continued trying to talk about the last few days and what I intend to talk about and clearly with (Spirit owner Bill Lynch's) actions, I think that that's a necessary conversation."[54]

---

54   Mandell, Nina. "NWSL's Washington Spirit prevent Megan Rapinoe's anthem protest," *USA Today*, September 7, 2016. www.usatoday.com/story/sports/soccer/2016/09/07/nwsl-national -anthem-prevent-megan-rapinoe-protest/89983278/

As frustrated as Rapinoe was by Lynch's language choices in the Spirit's statement, particularly his decision to call her protest a "hijacking" of the national anthem so close to the anniversary of September 11th, she also thought his decision undermined his own attempt to honor the flag.

"You talk about me disrespecting the flag, he didn't even give people a chance, give both teams a chance to even stand in front of it and show their respect. It's unbelievable."[55]

Complicating the situation with the Spirit was the fact that Lynch already had a reputation around the NWSL as one of the more conservative owners in the league. By 2016, the Washington Spirit never held a Pride Night at one of their games, an event that was common across the rest of the teams.

Rapinoe didn't shy away from connecting his reluctance to embrace LGBT visibility with the NWSL to his decision to play the anthem early, pointing at the Spirit's lack of Pride celebrations.

"I do think that Bill Lynch is homophobic," she said after the match.[56]

The national anthem at the Spirit game earned plenty of press coverage, positive and negative, but it also directly contributed to an exodus of Spirit players

---

55   Ibid.
56   Gibbs, Lindsay. "The hijacking Of Megan Rapinoe's national anthem protest," *ThinkProgress*, September 8, 2016. thinkprogress .org/washington-spirit-megan-rapinoe-protest-5b051600677b/

out of Washington, D.C., including Ali Krieger. As a Spirit player and captain, Krieger proved instrumental in organizing the players' disavowal of the early playing of the anthem.

Krieger, as well as Ashlyn Harris (who departed the Spirit one season before to play for the Orlando Pride), said the decision to play the anthem early opened their eyes—not just justifying their decisions to head to Orlando, but in how they understood Rapinoe's protest.

"A lot of us were just like, this is not where we want to be," Krieger said in 2019, during media availability with Harris before receiving an award from Athlete Ally.[57]

"All in all, the ownership did some shady things," Harris said. "It's not just about the queer community. It's about racial justice for all and having the freakin' anthem played when players are in the locker room. There's this shady shit all across the border and like, no one did anything about it."[58]

By September 15, Rapinoe was still going strong—this time in a US national team jersey. In a friendly (a match played outside of a tournament structure, but one that still counts for a team's international record) against

57   Gibbs, Lindsay. "'I was out of there': Ali Krieger and Ashlyn Harris open up about playing for homophobic NWSL owner," *Power Plays*, November 13, 2019. www.powerplays .news/p/i-was-out-of-there-ali-krieger-and
58   Ibid.

Thailand at Mapfre Stadium in Columbus, Ohio, Rapinoe once again knelt during the anthem on the sidelines. To her left, stood Alex Morgan. To her right, Meghan Klingenberg. Both stood, singing the anthem, with their hands placed over their hearts.

Rapinoe subbed on to start the second half; the US national team would go on to defeat Thailand 9–0 in the friendly. The win wasn't the story of the match, however, Rapinoe was.

That same night, US Soccer released a statement on her decision to protest while representing the United States as a member of the national team. In it, the federation defined the relationship between the players and staff of the national team and the national anthem: indeed, that there was a particular significance to the anthem as people represented their country on an international stage. US Soccer believed that players and staff should reflect upon "the liberties and freedom we all appreciate in this country"[59] during the anthem.

Because of this, the federation stated they had an expectation that all players and coaches would stand during the anthem, to also honor the flag.

US Soccer's statement overlooked that Rapinoe's actions were a reflection of Kaepernick's original protest, specifically made to point out that not every American enjoyed such liberties and freedom, particularly if they were Black or Brown.

---

59   US Soccer statement via Tweet, @SportsCenter, September 15, 2016. twitter.com/SportsCenter/status/776608084466827264

Even as Rapinoe made the decision to continue on, her own teammates were unsure of the consequences of her actions and what could possibly happen to them if they supported her.

"I don't know if I necessarily at that time agreed with her," defender Ali Krieger said in 2019. "Like, I support you because you're one of my best friends and I will support your views and your values, but I don't know if I can kneel with you, so to speak."[60]

As for goalkeeper Ashlyn Harris, the weeks of attention on Rapinoe and Kaepernick and the rest of the list of players opting to kneel were unsettling. Bringing that attention to the national team only made it harder to wrap her head around what Rapinoe was actually attempting to do. "When it first started, I think we were uncomfortable," she said. "That's what change is about, though."[61]

Defender Crystal Dunn detailed her discussions with Rapinoe in 2020, stating that she ultimately made the decision to stand for the anthem because she saw the amount of pushback from the federation. She was scared for her job, but she was also worried that the reaction would be different because of her race.

For Rapinoe, kneeling was an act of clear allyship. For Dunn, the implications were on a different scale. As

---

60   Gibbs, Lindsay. "'I was out of there': Ali Krieger and Ashlyn Harris open up about playing for homophobic NWSL owner," *Power Plays*, November 13, 2019. www.powerplays .news/p/i-was-out-of-there-ali-krieger-and
61   Ibid.

she said, "I'm scared that it's going to look differently if a black girl on the team kneels."[62]

With another friendly scheduled for September 18, this time in Atlanta against the Netherlands, all eyes were on Rapinoe and if she would continue despite all indications that there would be repercussions down the line for her.

At a press conference held on September 17, head coach Jill Ellis told the media that she understood Rapinoe's desire to talk about "hard social issues." There was no question that she respected it and supported it. She agreed that the conversation was a necessary one to have. The problem was that it was now happening in red, white, and blue—left unsaid was that it was inconvenient and distracting.

"Me personally, in this environment for a national team, I don't disassociate playing for your country. I think that's [the anthem] part of a national symbol. So in terms of standing for a national anthem, I think that's an expectation of a national team player," Ellis said.

She also expressed discomfort with the fact that Rapinoe was using the platform of the national team (and her club team) to continue her individual protest.

"For me personally, when it comes to utilizing a team platform when it comes to an individual agenda, yeah, I think I will always put team first, and would want the individuals to put team first."

62   Racism in Football || Roundtable Discussion After Black Lives Matter Protests, *YouTube*, uploaded by B/R Football, June 16, 2020 https://youtu.be/Dv0kvzVEvqc

Rapinoe kneeled, despite the statement from US Soccer, despite the expectations from Ellis. Once again, she did not start the match, but kneeled on the sidelines in the line of substitutes, and came on in the second half once again during the 3–1 win for the United States.

Rapinoe wouldn't play another minute in a national team kit for the rest of the year in the team's four remaining games.

By November, then–US Soccer President Sunil Gulati told reporter Paul Tenorio that there was a difference between the NWSL and the US national team when it came to protests of this nature.

Gulati also said that the right to free speech or the right to protest didn't really apply in Rapinoe's case, which was true enough. Rapinoe had the right to protest, but US Soccer as her employer also had the right to determine the consequences of such an action.

US Soccer's board felt there were two major factors for Rapinoe at that point: playing for country was not the same as playing for a domestic club, and playing for country meant expectations from the federation could— and would—be imposed on every player.

"There is a right to freedom of speech, she also has the obligations to putting on a national team uniform," Gulati said. "And we think those are pretty strong when you're representing the US national team and wearing the crest."[63]

---

63 Tenorio, Paul. "Sunil Gulati on Trump, 2026 World Cup Bid, USWNT CBA, Klinsmann, Pulisic, and NASL," *FourFourTwo*, November 11, 2016. https://www.fourfourtwo.com/us/features/sunil -gulati-trump-2026-world-cup-bid-uswnt-cba-pulisic

The US Soccer Board of Directors did feel strongly—enough to pass a new policy specifically inspired by Rapinoe's protests throughout the fall.

"All persons representing a Federation national team shall stand respectfully during the playing of national anthems at any event in which the Federation is represented," New Policy 604-1 read.

Rapinoe and the rest of the US national team said they would adhere to all the new policies adopted by the board.

"The federation was not very supportive, publicly or privately," Rapinoe wrote years later, in an article for *The Players' Tribune*. "I started getting left off rosters. It was never directly connected to my kneeling. They told me, 'You're not really at the level you need to be.'"[64]

Rapinoe barely made the national team roster for the 2016 Olympics after suffering an ACL injury in December of 2015—an injury she sustained on a subpar playing surface prior to a friendly in Hawaii. The players ultimately refused to play the match due to what they felt were unsafe playing conditions, and the game was cancelled. These frustrations over field conditions were not new, and would also come up time and time again in the players' fight for equal pay and equal respect.

But that injury and Sweden's upset of the national team in Rio for the team's earliest exit from an Olympic

---

64 Rapinoe, Megan. "You Can't Get Rid of Your Girl That Easily," *The Players' Tribune*, June 23, 2019. www.theplayerstribune.com /en-us/articles/megan-rapinoe-united-states-world-cup-youre-not -gonna-get-rid-of-your-girl-that-easily

tournament ever meant that Rapinoe felt she was on the outside looking in. Choosing to kneel at that particular moment in time, when her roster spot was in question like never before, meant that there were potentially real consequences from a career standpoint.

Rapinoe felt like she was being blackballed by the federation, essentially. That they were hoping she would retire, or at the very least, accept that she wasn't about to be called up for as long as she kept up her political activism.

"I wasn't gonna fade away," Rapinoe wrote. "Tough shit."[65]

Rapinoe did stop kneeling, but she also didn't fade away. Her career faltered for a few months, but she did eventually make her return in a more meaningful way, becoming an essential part of the starting forward line on the wing beside Alex Morgan and Tobin Heath.

With a year's distance between her and the choice to kneel, having lived through the backlash and with the phone calls calling her into national teams having dried up and then starting to come again, she didn't look back on her experience thinking it could have gone another way—beyond, perhaps, the NWSL and US Soccer being willing to engage in the conversation in a more meaningful way.

A year later, Rapinoe didn't think she had made some breakthrough and discovered a perfect way to protest. She didn't think it existed. But she also decided that

---

65 Ibid.

she wouldn't have changed her approach or her actions. She felt she had done her part to force the conversation, even if the conversation hadn't exactly resolved itself in any sort of meaningful way, and had pushed as far as she could within the bounds she was given. And most importantly, she knew her own heart and her own mind.

By the time the 2019 World Cup rolled around, Rapinoe figured out a compromise for the national anthem before every game, whether for club or country.

For every game—now as she was starting for the US national team in the build-up to the summer's tournament, Rapinoe stood. But she did not sing. She did not put her hand over her heart. She kept her hands behind her back, sometimes she bowed her head. She used the time to reflect.

In the article announcing that Rapinoe earned the honor of the *Sports Illustrated* Sportsperson of the Year in 2019, Jenny Vrentas wrote that Rapinoe sometimes let "the names of people of color who have unjustly lost their lives run through her mind. Trayvon Martin. Michael Brown. Tamir Rice. She stops herself. She doesn't want to seem like she's leveraging their names."[66]

In the end, her career has taken a different path than Kaepernick's, who's still looking for a full-time NFL job

---

66   Vrentas, Jenny. "2019 Sportsperson of the Year: Megan Rapinoe," *Sports Illustrated*, December 9, 2019. www.si.com /sportsperson/2019/12/09/megan-rapinoe-2019-sportsperson -of-the-year

in 2019. But her path wasn't without consequences, even as she found tremendous personal success three years later.

The criticism never went away, especially in the summer of 2019—not just over her decision to protest in the past, her unwillingness to go to the White House, but the way she chose to celebrate goals, over how she stood for the anthem. She was called anti-American, accused of not loving the country.

Add in the fact that it was the Women's World Cup, the USWNT's battle over equal pay, the background of social movements for women's rights coming to the forefront over the past few years, and Rapinoe—that "pink-haired, unapologetically flaming gay lesbian"— became not just a focal point for her political beliefs in the summer of 2019, but a reflection, perhaps even a paradigm of this particular moment in time.

Even though she ultimately chose to follow US Soccer's rule to stand for the anthem, she found her own way to stay true to her values.

"I'll probably never put my hand over my heart," Rapinoe said in 2019.

"I'll probably never sing the national anthem again."[67]

A year later, the act of kneeling changed. It remained a protest, but by 2020, too many athletes to count had joined Kaepernick and Rapinoe in this act of protest. The list of names had gotten longer, and a larger swath of

---

67 Bushnell, Henry. "Megan Rapinoe is a 'walking protest,'" Yahoo! Sports, May 13, 2019. sports.yahoo.com/megan-rapinoe-is-a-walking -protest-162416461.html

white America finally understood that kneeling during the anthem had never been about the flag or the military, but about the lack of rights and freedom for Black and Brown people in this country. Kneeling addressed police brutality, kneeling addressed systemic injustices.

While Megan Rapinoe did not choose to play in the NWSL Challenge Cup, held in the summer of 2020 by the league to safely play games in the midst of the COVID-19 pandemic, her fellow players followed her example. At the same times the games were played, the country was also in the midst of grappling with its own legacy of white supremacy and police brutality—issues Rapinoe and Kaepernick had wanted to highlight in 2016.

The NWSL front office chose to continue playing the national anthem in the summer of 2020, even as no outside fans were allowed to attend games, and the vast majority of players chose to kneel. For the first match of the Challenge Cup, every player who started the match between the North Carolina Courage and Portland Thorns FC—one of the league's strongest rivalries with no love lost between the two sides—kneeled in unison and issued a joint statement in support of the Black Lives Matter movement.

The work is not complete, but the movement spread—this time, Crystal Dunn, who plays for the Thorns in the NWSL, did not worry about her job security or how it would look for a Black player to kneel.

She simply did so, arms locked with her teammates on either side.

The NWSL wasn't the only organization working to undo some of the harm caused by shutting down legitimate avenues of protest, even if there were technical arguments from governing bodies like the league or US Soccer to say they could put a stop to them.

In June 2020, the US Soccer Federation repealed its anthem policy. The federation's statement upon the repeal was to the point: the policy was wrong. The federation acknowledged they had not done enough to listen to their own players and staff not just on their expectations for the anthem but also on the issues of police brutality and systemic oppression, and they issued an apology.

"We apologize to our players—especially our Black players—staff, fans, and all who support eradicating racism," their statement read. As of the summer of 2020, the federation will allow players to determine their own actions without standing in the way.

"We are here for our players and are ready to support them in elevating their efforts to achieve social justice. We cannot change the past, but we can make a difference in the future."[68]

---

68 "US Soccer Board of Directors Votes to Repeal National Anthem Policy," US Soccer, June 10, 2020. ussoccer.com/stories/2020/06/us-soccer-board-of-directors-votes-to-repeal-policy-national-anthem-policy

CHAPTER FIVE

Know your worth. If others don't see it, take matters into your own hands.

"This is who I am, I'm damn proud of it, and hopefully you are too."

MEGAN RAPINOE HAS BEEN OPEN about who she is and open about her values as a human over the course of her career. Those values drove both her image and her public profile. She's always possessed firm opinions about her value—not for her performance on the field but about her marketability as both an individual professional athlete and as part of the US national team.

The state of the financial side of women's soccer has changed fairly drastically even over the last decade. Even as Rapinoe got her first major dose of fame following the 2011 World Cup, experts still expressed major doubts about the players actually capitalizing on the attention via new endorsement deals.

"US Women's Soccer Team Not That Marketable," declared an article on CNBC, only days after the national team defeated Brazil in the epic quarterfinal match, via Rapinoe and Wambach's last-ditch goal and penalty kicks, before the final was even played.

"The problem is that when the final World Cup game is played on Sunday, the ladies have a ghost of a stage to return to," wrote Darren Rovell.[69]

While the tone of the article was dismissive, Rovell's point wasn't entirely inaccurate—in 2012, the professional league at the time, Women's Professional Soccer, was actually only months away from folding.

"If they win out, there's going to be a halo for them and some additional endorsement opportunities," Peter Stern of Strategic, a New York–based marketing firm, said in the article. "But they clearly have to find a way to stay in the spotlight. The Dream Team went out and won on the Olympic level, but then they returned to the highest level in the world in the NBA. These women don't have that."[70]

That same marketing expert said most brands' best hope of success with someone from the 2011 team, such

69   Rovell, Darren. "US Women's Soccer Team Not That
Marketable," CNBC, July 13, 2011. www.cnbc.com/id/43738829
70   Ibid.

as goalkeeper Hope Solo (Rapinoe wasn't even on their radar as a possibility), would actually be reality television, instead of professional women's soccer.

Either way, Rovell concluded that the team had to win the World Cup to find commercial success, and even if they did, the team would likely still be left out in the cold by the larger world of marketing, unimpressed with women's sports as a general concept.

As Rapinoe was working with her team behind the scenes on what being openly gay would mean for her career, immediately following the 2011 World Cup, ahead of the 2012 Olympic Games, this was the state of thinking around the national team—and like everyone else, she lost the platform of a professional league as well.

Even with uncertain repercussions, Rapinoe still made the call to come out, a decision that she never regretted—and actually linked to an improved performance from 2011 on, including a gold medal–winning performance at the 2012 Olympics.

The 2011 World Cup, the 2012 Olympics—these two tournaments began the modern era of the US women's national team, and also helped ensure the creation of the longest-lasting professional league in America, the National Women's Soccer League in 2013. By 2015, when the United States finally won the World Cup again for the first time since 1999, there was more meaningful infrastructure in place to allow the sport to grow, even if that growth was still, in many ways, limited by external factors.

"In America, women's soccer has totally exploded in this amazing way," Rapinoe wrote in 2016. "It's also exploded in this way that suits the status quo. The media attention on the team is so much more than in the past, but it still needs to be diversified in my opinion. Women are still so objectified in the media and sports is no exception."[71]

Rapinoe grew frustrated with the willingness that ad companies had only embraced objectification, rather than all dimensions of women athletes, particularly their strength.

On the flip side, Rapinoe understood that the 2011 World Cup in particular helped fans understand the sport in a way they hadn't before, that the Brazil game, and subsequent loss to Japan in the final, likely helped women's soccer escape the shadow of the 1999 World Cup a bit in America.

"I felt like after Mia [Hamm] and those guys retired, it took a hard dip for the team and the popularity of women's soccer," Rapinoe said after they did finally take home the trophy in Canada. "After that, it's been all uphill. Coming home and having the support we did—and we didn't even win!—that was very telling for us. I think it shows the growth in fandom, too. People start to understand more than winning and losing. Have you seen that kind of growth in the game since you started playing as a kid?

---

71 Rapinoe, Megan. "Tomboys," *The Players' Tribune*, April 7, 2016. www.theplayerstribune.com/en-us/articles/megan-rapinoe-uswnt -soccer-tomboys

The understanding of the nuances of soccer in America? It's everywhere. It's catching on. Is it the NFL yet? No."[72]

Rapinoe would still have some of those same lingering frustrations by the end of the next World Cup cycle, even after another tournament win and with the continued growth of the NWSL. Still, the sponsorship and marketing landscape of women's soccer was light-years ahead—though obviously still with plenty of room for improvement in how various influencing organizations (the league, the media, etc.) represented the athletes. Rapinoe was one of the top players to benefit, even as she positioned herself with strong political views.

Even before the 2019 World Cup, Nike tried to push the narrative of their increased investment into women's soccer. The company sponsored Rapinoe since 2009, and watched her role in the growth of the sport in America—but for the World Cup, they had much larger plans.

"From the time we began working on the Women's World Cup kits three years ago, we believed 2019 would be a tipping point for women's football (soccer)," Amy Montagne, VP, GM of Global Categories at Nike, told Forbes while pointing to both the rise of women's sports as well as the health and wellness movement.[73]

72   Koczwara, Kevin. "An Interview with Megan Rapinoe," Believer Mag, October 1, 2015. believermag.com/an-interview-with-megan -rapinoe/

73   Kidd, Robert. "Why Nike Believes 2019 Is a Tipping Point for Women's Soccer," Forbes, April 7, 2019. forbes.com/sites /robertkidd/2019/04/07/why-nike-believes-2019-is-a-tipping-point -for-womens-soccer/

It wasn't just the landscape of women's soccer and increased investment from brands that changed over the past decade, it was the entire way that people related to these brands themselves.

According to a 2018 report from Edelman, a public relations and marketing consultancy firm, the rise of the "Belief-Driven Buyer" was truly underway, with almost two-thirds of their survey's respondents saying they "choose, switch to or boycott a brand based on its stand on societal issues."[74]

The report concluded that consumers are voting with their dollars more than their actual votes. Brands, after all, are hyper conscious of what's influencing people to buy their products. Politicians might not answer to the very people who elected them, and if they do, the firm still suggested that consumers found them ineffective.

But brands could be pressured in other ways, from the supply chain on down. Consumers encourage, even force, these companies to become advocates and allies. "This is a new relationship between company and consumer—purchase is premised on a brand's willingness to live by its values, operate with purpose, and if necessary make the leap into activism," the report concludes.[75]

And what player on the national team and in the NWSL loudly lived by her values better than Megan

74 Edelman Earned Report Executive Summary, October 2018.
edelman.com/sites/g/files/aatuss191/files/2018-10/2018_Edelman
_Earned_Brand_Executive_Summary_Brochure.pdf
75 Ibid.

Rapinoe? And it wasn't even that potential consumers simply looked to brands to take a stand—53 percent of respondents for that same survey thought that brands could actually do more than the government itself to fix social issues.

The trend is one that's only going to increase with time.

"Articulate, honest and authoritative about subjects that matter, the complexion of the ideal athlete brand ambassador has evolved," wrote Sam Carp in an article about Rapinoe's marketability post–World Cup. "Sport has always been a microcosm of wider society, but rarely have those that compete been so willing to have a say in how that society is shaped. Theirs are the causes that brands will be clamoring to get behind."[76]

One of Rapinoe's key sponsors over the course of her career, Nike, hoped to lead the way with a number of campaigns featuring Colin Kaepernick. "Believe in something," the copy read. "Even if it means sacrificing everything." And while some boycotted, Nike's stock surged, adding about $6 billion in value to the company.

So ultimately, going all in on Rapinoe—that same pink-haired, unapologetically flaming gay lesbian, one who kneeled during the anthem like Kaepernick, who was suing her own federation for equal pay—wasn't a

76 Carp, Sam. "Megan Rapinoe, athlete activism, and the changing face of marketability," *SportsPro*, July 17, 2019. www.sportspromedia .com/opinion/megan-rapinoe-donald-trump-athlete-activism-brand -ambassadors-marketability

hard call for the company. They were there the entire time, after all.

Other brands have been catching up to Nike, not just on the women's soccer front, but when it comes to Rapinoe as well. Visa has increased their sponsorship on the women's side across the board, and added Rapinoe to their list of sponsored athletes in May 2019.

Rapinoe treated this sponsorship as a two-way street, and used that new relationship to push for her own agenda with Visa, and what she thought they were capable of changing across the marketplace and the sports world.

"To be able to not only partner with brands, but to help influence the way they see the world, the way they interact in the space around women's equality—and just opportunity for women—is really important to me," Rapinoe told *Ad Age* in an interview[77] after Visa launched their 2020 Olympic roster of sponsorships.

Rapinoe also spoke with Visa about their sponsorship with US Soccer—a key detail of their long-term partnership was that at least half of the resources allocated were required to go to women within the federation, including both players and coaches.

"All the time we talk about what's going to influence people?" Rapinoe asked hypothetically. "What's going to influence the (International Olympic Committee),

77   Doland, Angela, "Megan Rapinoe, Simone Biles and Katie Ledecky are on Visa's Roster of Athletes for the 2020 Olympics," *Ad Age*, November 14, 2019. adage.com/article/special-report-olympics /megan-rapinoe-simone-biles-and-katie-ledecky-are-visas-roster -athletes-2020-olympics/2214951

what's going to influence all of these big federations and governing bodies? It's money, obviously, and ads and sponsorships."[78]

Chris Curtin, Visa's chief brand and innovation marketing officer, said that the company was tracking the landscape of the sponsorship market around women's sports.

"We believe in equality and our sponsorships reflect that," Curtin said. "While the investment and enthusiasm around the globe for women's sports continues to rise, we recognize there is still more work to be done, and we will work with our partners to help promote equality."[79]

Even Curtin mentioned that historically brands had not invested as much in the marketing and promotion of women's sports, not to the levels they deserved.

By leveraging her relationships with both new and old sponsors, and even potential ones, Rapinoe has been fond of making sure that she's in the room—and more importantly, as of 2019, making sure the results of those conversations are shared for accountability.

"I think you probably know this at this point, but a good public calling out never hurt anybody," Rapinoe said. "I personally like doing that, because it makes people accountable. I can go into all these rooms and have all the conversations I want, and we can sit in

---

78   Ibid.
79   Linehan, Meg. "In the glow of a World Cup win, the sponsorship landscape for US women's soccer is more important than ever," *The Athletic*, July 29, 2019. theathletic.com/1104037/

there, and we can say how important it is to support women's sports, and yadda yadda yadda, we've been doing that for years. We've been in a million of those rooms."[80]

For brands that talk a big game, then never take the leap with investments, she's decided she's done letting that slide.

"Your silence doesn't get to be silence anymore," she said. "Your silence is going to say something."[81]

In 2019, Rapinoe was also tapped by Budweiser for a campaign as part of their new sponsorship with the National Women's Soccer League, inked right at the close of the World Cup. Their first message as sponsors urged fans to continue watching the players in the league; their second was actually a far more interesting move as a brand. Budweiser directly called on other brands to also sponsor the NWSL, with Rapinoe front and center of both the video and print ads.

"Today, Budweiser is calling for more brands to join them as official supporters of the NWSL," Rapinoe said in the video spot. "Believe them when they say, it's worth it. Yeah, these fans drink beer. But they also use their phones for texting, and headphones for music. They eat snacks and their pets do, too."[82]

---

80   Linehan, Meg. "'A good public calling out never hurt anybody': Megan Rapinoe on the ways Budweiser is pushing the NWSL forward," *The Athletic*, November 6, 2019. theathletic.com/1356886/
81   Ibid.
82   "It's Worth Supporting," *YouTube*, uploaded by Budweiser, October 24, 2019. https://youtu.be/EjrjDt6C_r0

Again, like Nike, Budweiser leaned on greater social concepts, even in this campaign, aiming for those belief-driven buyers, ones that would be paying particular attention to Rapinoe.

Rapinoe's voiceover finished with this premise: "The more support the league gets, the more the world will watch. The more the world watches, the closer we get to an equal playing field. And that's something we can all cheers to."[83]

Rapinoe's goal went beyond greater financial stability and awareness for the NWSL, she also hoped to upgrade the messaging around women's soccer in general.

"Hopefully other brands get involved, and realize you can be cheeky and fun and get involved with it," she said, "and ultimately do something that's really great and impactful, and we feel like it has a good opportunity for return for the sponsors, as well."

Rapinoe has been waiting on that shift, has been watching how men's sports (the NBA has been a particular reference point for her, rather than MLS or other men's soccer leagues) are presented, how male athletes are not bogged down with the same expectations of being role models.

"It depends on what kind of culture you want to create, but with soccer, we want the diversity, we want younger people, we want the rebel a little bit, we want this undercurrent crowd," she said. "We want people who are working and spending their own money on what

---

83 Ibid.

they want to do, and we need to make it cool. Having a stadium full of seven-year-olds is not cool. You need the seven-year-olds there, but you also need everybody else to make the environment what it needs to be in order for the support to succeed."

When it came to the NWSL in particular, both from a league-wide perspective and with varying results from team to team, Rapinoe particularly saw a real lagging effort to break down those same old-school stereotypes of women's soccer players.

"I think the league has actually been marketed exactly the way that it's seeing its own players," she said. "'Great, you guys want to be role models, great, you work hard, great, this and that,'" she continued, her voice dripping with a saccharine sarcasm.

"It's like, 'No, actually, we're bad-ass professional athletes.'"[84]

It's not just the league that plays a role in how the players are represented, there's the national team itself, brands, the media, even how the fans interact. Rapinoe has never been very shy about making herself available for interviews; she's never been shy about sharing what she's thinking. But as much as she can present her own truth via interviews and press conferences and speeches, frequently, her words are interpreted by someone else

---

84 Linehan, Meg. "'A good public calling out never hurt anybody': Megan Rapinoe on the ways Budweiser is pushing the NWSL forward," *The Athletic*, November 6, 2019. theathletic.com/1356886/

before they get to her final audience. (That's exactly what's happening in this book, after all.)

Rapinoe was asked in France at a press conference during the World Cup about if she'd like to look out into the crowded room and see more faces that belonged to women and to people of color.

"As much as we love seeing all your men's faces, the more women, the better I would say," she answered. "Of course, we want to get more women asking the questions to tell the stories from a different perspective, but also just giving people more opportunities, I think overall, will help tell a more complete story of the women's game and of women's sports in general. For us female athletes, I think it tells a more complete story when we have a diverse group of people telling that story for us."

Rapinoe spoke in 2019 about balancing her relationships with brands and media against her own bodily autonomy and personal image. She said that over the course of her career, she became more confident in her own voice and her own creative vision, compared to earlier in her career. As a younger player, she followed commands to "Smile! Do this! Blah, blah, blah," as she put it.

She pointed to her participation in the *Sports Illustrated* swimsuit edition in 2019 as something she could take greater control over.

"I did the swimsuit cover in like essentially nothing," she said at an event with Gloria Steinem (much more on that later), "but it doesn't mean that you can't look beautiful, or you can't look sexy or whatever these things are, but I want to make sure that I'm doing it for me and for the people that I care about as well. So I think there's, it's sort of the intention that you bring behind it, and there's definitely been times where I'm like, 'No, I'm not doing that, it sounds ridiculous.' Being able to stand up and say that and to push back on different creatives and what it's actually saying, what message is it portraying, is it true to me, is it true to what I'm saying in the broader worldview that I want to live in. I think that when you don't do that it's just, it just doesn't come off as authentic, and then the whole thing's a flop, so it's not really worth doing anyways. So really trying to be true to yourself and understand what you're trying to put out there and then sort of demand that from the companies of people or whoever it is that you're working with."

Ultimately, Rapinoe has still felt forced to take matters into her own hands, even at this point in her career.

"You have to market yourself the way you want to be seen, and for the future that you want to have," Rapinoe said. "It's just been, honestly, such a lack of creativity and awareness about where we want to go. Just very boring."

There is one way she's been able to have complete and direct control over her own image, in addition to taking an active role with her sponsorships—she's also been involved in her own business ventures, most notable, a small family-run company with her twin sister Rachael.

The two of them founded Rapinoe SC in 2015 as their catch-all base of operations: running soccer camps for youth players, and a small apparel line that they designed. The motto of the company had always been, "Be Your Best You," one that appeared on plenty of their shirts.

As their official site described their motto, "Being Your Best You transcends far beyond the pitch. We care about the development of people of all ages and backgrounds. We want to help everyone reach their full potential, both athletically and personally. The Rapinoe brand is for everyone, because we are all in this quest together."[85]

That's not to say running a business has been easy for either of them. After Rapinoe kneeled in 2016, Rachael said that the Rapinoe SC received constant emails for almost a year. Camp registrations were harder to come by. The apparel line sales dried up. It took them over a year to recover.

Even as they built the business back up, and saw some additional interest thanks to the 2019 World Cup, ultimately both moved onto new ventures and the Rapinoe Club was shuttered in early 2020. Rachael moved on to Mendi, a company that sells CBD products targeted for athlete recovery. Megan was signed as Mendi's first athlete ambassador, as well as serving as a board advisor and strategic partner.

In an interview posted on the Mendi website, Rapinoe acknowledged all of the factors that went into her decision to partner with the company and her twin sister. "Cannabis in general has always been a very politicized

85 Rapinoe SC, LLC homepage. www.rapinoe.us/rapinoe-sc/

issue," Megan Rapinoe said, "especially with the legalization of it. I find it to be really important to be extremely
thoughtful and careful about who I'm partnering with.
There are a lot of social justice implications, a lot of status
quo implications."

She pointed to the company's intentions, but also that
Mendi was a female-founded company and female-run.
For Rapinoe, the real key to her decision was thoughtful-
ness and impact.[86]

Obviously, with the company selling CBD, there was
also reason for her to go on record about legalization as
well.

"As a company, we want to ensure that Mendi has
diverse representation in our workforce, good working
conditions with our partners, and we use Mendi to educate the general public about CBD and cannabis use,"
she said. "It is no secret that many people have spent
years in jail for cannabis, of those people a dispropor-
tionate percentage are people of color. We will use this
company and our platform to raise awareness and fight
for the legalization of CBD and cannabis everywhere."[87]

Rapinoe wasn't only working with her sister though.
She formed a new company of her own, alongside
USWNT teammates Christen Press, Tobin Heath, and
former US national team player Meghan Klingenberg

---

86   "It's Time to Speak Up," Mendi. https://themendico.com/our
-interview-with-soccer-star-and-mendi-athlete-ambassador-megan
-rapinoe
87   Ibid.

in 2019. Re—inc was founded as a "purposeful lifestyle brand," but also one that sold fairly expensive athleisure apparel as well.

Their first clothing launch was described on their website with lofty goals: clothes, after all, help people define who they are. The company leaned into this, embracing expression, rejecting gender norms. The color choices were intentional as well, reflecting the red, white, and blue of America, but instead of bold, vibrant colors, Rapinoe and co. muted them. Jewel tones became earth tones.

If brands had new expectations from their customers to take a stand according to recent research, re—inc took things a step farther and had expectations of those who wound up buying their products.

The product description asked people "to reflect on what it truly means to be patriotic and how best to represent our country. Patriotism redefined."[88]

That sort of language matched how the four players described the company itself, one they formed to "boldly reimagine the status quo—championing equity, creativity, progress, and art."

For all the idealistic concepts behind re—inc, there was a disconnect in the accessibility, when it came to product pricing.

As Sydney Kuntz wrote for *SB Nation*, the company may have been pricing out those who could have found

---

88   Product description available on re—inc website, re-website.com

greater meaning in nonconforming clothing, "people who already have enough barriers dressing comfortably."[89]

At the same time, Kuntz didn't want to lay all of the various faults of capitalism and athlete-driven fashion directly at Rapinoe, Press, Heath, and Klingenberg's feet. And while there was a disconnect between the athletes' call for equal pay and the pricing of their products, Kuntz also struggled to hold this pricing against them, too, when re—inc was additional work: "It's also hard to judge when these athletes deserve more attention and pay for the work that they do, especially when their messaging is so powerful."[90]

Even if the execution wasn't perfect—streetwear does typically carry higher price tags—Rapinoe told *The Wall Street Journal* that she viewed the company as another vehicle for equality. The equal pay fight was years in the making, and still wasn't settled. Rapinoe and the three other players were looking for something they could control.

"So what can we do? Maybe we can actually start a company, run it totally different," Rapinoe said. "And maybe we're just a small company now and we're only affecting a few people. But what if we inspire another company to do that? What if we inspire existing companies?

89   Kuntz, Sydney. "Megan Rapinoe's gender-neutral clothing line would be great, if the joggers weren't $150," *SB Nation*, November 12, 2019. www.sbnation.com/2019/11/12/20961569/megan-rapinoes-re-inc-clothing-line-tobin-heath
90   Ibid.

"What if we inspire a community to actually do everything different than what we've been fighting against for the whole time?"[91]

All four players were on the 2015 World Cup squad; all four thought that the win failed to translate into lasting personal financial success.

"You just couldn't help but think, 'Well, there's just a lot missing here,'" Rapinoe told Rachel Bachman. "Sort of a disappointment and a yearning for more. Knowing that we're just not capitalizing on it, and we have no way."[92]

Part of that fight against the federation resulted in some of the players' likeness rights being returned to them in the most recent collective bargaining agreement— rights that the USWNT Players Association was in charge of maximizing via new partnerships, ones that picked up plenty of extra revenue.

Rapinoe and the rest of the national team were finally able to earn money from USA jerseys being sold, ones that featured their names and numbers on the back. There were new ways to create t-shirts, bobbleheads, other merchandise. And there was demand, especially in 2019.

"In 2015, the licensing revenue was $0 to the Players Association," Becca Roux, the director of the USWNT Players Association, told *Yahoo! Sports* in 2019. "Now

91   Bachman, Rachel. "US Women's Soccer Players to Launch Business," The Wall Street Journal, May 26, 2019. www.wsj.com /articles/u-s-womens-soccer-players-to-launch-business-11558872001
92   Ibid.

we're on pace for $1 million this year. That's a huge dif-ference, but we're still barely scratching the surface. We had no sales data going into this World Cup to attract these licensees and get on the floor of these major retailers, but it has done well."[93]

Press, also involved in re—inc, earned first-hand experience from the players association making the most of their licensing rights.

"We have a very special group of players since 2015 that worked really hard to reestablish our players' association and run it like a business," Press told the *LA Times*. "While we were empowering ourselves and believing in our own value, the kickback that we got was this amazing learning opportunity."[94]

US Soccer chose not to pursue that very value of the US national team. Even without data, there was belief that the players and the team was marketable, that there was demand. Through personal business ventures, the efforts of the players association, brand campaigns, and ticket sales, Rapinoe and the United States national team proved there was a value, and their values as players,

93   Murray, Caitlin. "How USWNT is successfully monetizing its image rights after being told they had 'no value,'" *Yahoo! Sports*, September 3, 2019. sports.yahoo.com/how-uswnt-is-successfully -monetizing-its-image-rights-after-being-told-they-had-no-value -174754539.html

94   Shaikin, Bill. "US women's soccer players start to cash in on licensing -- that's using your bobblehead," *The Los Angeles Times*, August 2, 2019. www.latimes.com/sports/soccer/story/2019-08-02 /us-womens-soccer-marketing

fighting for equality, were just as important in the marketability of the team.

It wasn't just the national team—Rapinoe took control of her own value at every level of her career, from personal brands and commercial ventures to owning how she's marketed as a professional player to fighting to control the rights for her and her teammates. Even as potential sponsors and the teams she played for failed to fully imagine the value of women's soccer or her as an athlete, Rapinoe sought to reimagine her image—from role model to bad-ass, a player who could keep both her own interests and the next generation in mind at the same time. She didn't just know her worth, but she worked to gain full control over her own destiny.

CHAPTER SIX

Stand your ground on equality, always

"We won't accept anything less than equal pay."

RAPINOE AND THE PLAYERS OF the US national team didn't begin their fight for equal pay when they filed a gender discrimination lawsuit in federal court against the US Soccer Federation in March of 2019—even before she and four other members of the team filed a complaint with the Equal Employment Opportunity Commission in 2016.

For as long as the women's national team has existed as a part of the US Soccer Federation since the mid-1980s, the players have pushed for additional resources and better pay, especially following success at major international tournaments like the World Cup. While previous rosters on the US national team did not quite take the full-on activist tack of Rapinoe and the current generation of players, there were two major incidents in the USWNT's history that help illuminate the current fight for equal pay—and show how history has repeated itself time and time again when it comes to gender equality and US Soccer.

In 1995, nine players—Michelle Akers, Joy Fawcett, Julie Foudy, Carin Gabarra, Mia Hamm, Kristine Lilly, Carla Overbeck, Briana Scurry, and Tisha Venturini—all of whom were on the '95 World Cup roster, refused new contract offers from US Soccer ahead of the 1996 Olympic Games, held on American soil. The new contracts only offered bonuses if the women won gold in the upcoming Olympics, whereas the men's national team earned bonuses as long as they medaled.

US Soccer, in response, locked them out from attending the first training camp of 1996.

According to US Soccer statements at the time, all nine of the players "were under contract in 1995 and each was extended an opportunity to return as full-time national team players through September 1996."[95] The federation was also disappointed by the players' unwillingness to accept the contracts on face value.

Then–secretary general of USSF, Hank Steinbrecher, told the *LA Times* that the federation "made good-faith

---

95   Jones, Grahame. "Women Soccer Players Boycott Olympic Camp: Atlanta Games: Dispute involving top US players hinges on rejection of contract offers." The Los Angeles Times, December 6, 1995. www.latimes.com/archives/la-xpm-1995-12-06-sp-10918-story.html

offers to continue to make our players the highest-compensated women's national team players in the world." He also pointed to the investment the federation made into the team ahead of the 1995 World Cup and the 1996 Olympics, "an unprecedented #3.4-million commitment."[96]

The *LA Times* reported that the players were making "as much as $80,000 or $90,000 a year" from their time with US Soccer, though the story did not state those figures included additional income from sponsors and not just their actual national team salary.

US Soccer's response—from the reactionary quotes to the lockout—was actually only helping the players in their fight for more respect, even if it was unintentional.

Ellen Zavian, an attorney who was helping the nine players with their contracts and who had plenty of experience on NFL contracts, said in 2019 that she planned for that level of conflict between the players and their own federation.

"I very much wanted a lockout, because the public looks at strikes as players whining," Zavian told WBUR. "And I had been through an '87 strike with NFL players where there were scabs. So from that experience, I realized that a lockout actually brings the media and the fans much more supportive of the players."[97]

---

96 Ibid.
97 Shulman, Ken. "'Let's Move On This': The '99 US Women's National Team's Fight For Equality," WBUR, June 7, 2019. www.wbur .org/onlyagame/2019/06/07/lilly-foudy-lockout-world-cup-team-usa

In fact, Steinbrecher and the federation essentially ripped up the contract offers for the nine players, telling them the only way they could return to the national team was if head coach Tony DiCicco called them up on a per diem basis.

The request for a bonus for any Olympic medal seemed to have particularly struck a sore spot with Steinbrecher and US Soccer, despite the USWNT winning the 1991 World Cup, then following it up with a third-place finish in Sweden in 1995. Perhaps it was because the 1996 Olympics would be held in Atlanta and national pride on the line, perhaps it was because it was actually the first time women's soccer would be featured during the Games.

Either way, Steinbrecher was not impressed by the women asking for their bonus structure to match the men's national team.

"We cannot reward mediocrity," he said. "It seems some players are more concerned about how green their shoes are, instead of bringing home the gold."

Years before the US women's national team player association would exist, these nine players realized the power in standing together and earning public good will. US Soccer did eventually back down; the players returned, and the team was guaranteed compensation for a gold, silver, or bronze finish. But in the summer of 1996, the US women's national team won gold at home—a win not only for the future of the program, but a launching pad for the country to host the 1999 World Cup.

Of course, the US would go on to win that World Cup in the most dramatic fashion at the Rose Bowl—but the team also immediately followed up this success with a boycott as they protested for better wages from US Soccer.

Twenty players from the World Cup roster played for the federation via a run of short-term contracts post-'99 World Cup that would carry them through a couple of months of games, before another short-term contract would be drawn up. Both sides were planning to work together on something more long-term that would carry the team through the 2000 Olympics, at minimum.

Ahead of a small tournament held in Australia in January 2020, US Soccer offered up the same terms for another short-term contract that would last through February, which would pay each player $6,300 for the scheduled games, and would not offer any bonuses. The players countered, asking for $5,000 a month, with match bonuses of $2,000 per game. The federation simply pointed once again at their offer of $6,300 total.

The 20 players refused to accept the original offer, skipping out on the Australia tournament, to which US Soccer sent a roster of younger players. This time, the federation didn't want a repeat of how the 1995 labor situation played out.

Steinbrecher was still serving as secretary general of US Soccer, and still unimpressed by the lengths the women were prepared to go to for better pay. He denied that the twenty players boycotting the tournament was even a boycott. "They're currently unemployed," he told *Soccer America* in 2000. "They chose not to play for their country."[98]

By 1999, the players of the women's national team successfully fought for better wages, for additional bonuses, for severance pay and paid pregnancy leave. But after the World Cup win on home soil, in which the team didn't only perform on the field, but helped promote the game to a national audience, the players felt they deserved a raise.

The federation disagreed, once again pointing to the financial losses on the women's side, as well as the lack of a women's professional league that would provide additional income for the players.

"We're not going to mortgage our future for one team," Steinbrecher said in 2000.

"In the absence of a weekly league, they look to us for a weekly paycheck," he continued. "We have prepared that team very well and invested very heavily in them, more so than any team in the world. But that's not a tenable position for a not-for-profit organization like the Federation."

The federation was also more than willing to ignore the public support for the players, even after the huge popularity boost given by two major international tournaments in America.

---

98 "Women's boycott: behind the pay dispute," *Soccer America*, January 10, 2000. www.socceramerica.com/publications/article/14512/womens-boycott-behind-the-pay-dispute.html

"It's a very vogue thing to be on the side of the women on this," Steinbrecher said. "We're going to do what we think is best regardless of what the media has to say or uninformed people have to say."

By the end of January, however, the federation and players came to terms on a new long-term contract that would last through the 2004 Olympics—one that heavily favored the demands of the players. This was in part thanks to the national team players getting buy-in from the younger players, including those who travelled to Australia to play in the January tournament, to refuse call-ups from US Soccer until a new contract was in place.

Under the new contract, the players were guaranteed a minimum salary of $5,000 a month, but also included various appearance fees and bonuses—including a $2,000 bonus for every match leading up to the Olympics.

"I think we've worked out something that will help the future of women's soccer," USWNT captain Carla Overbeck told the *New York Times*. "It's unfortunate it had to come to this. We've always wanted to play. I'm proud our younger players were on board with us as far as not playing until the contract was worked out."[99]

Sixteen years after Overbeck felt her squad helped the future of women's soccer, progress was certainly made,

99 Longman, Jere. "SOCCER; Women's Team Ends Boycott, Agreeing to a Contract," The *New York Times*, January 20, 2000. www.nytimes.com/2000/01/30/sports/soccer-women-s-team-ends-boycott-agreeing-to-a-contract.html

but not as much as that team may have hoped for back in their day.

"I don't want to speak for the players, but my sense is 'Really, we're still having this conversation?'" Julie Foudy told the *Associated Press* in 2016 after the players filed their EEOC complaint. "Our fight was, it would be nice to get more than $10 per diem and that was it. It's much different and nuanced than years ago."[100]

While the fight is different, the general approach to how to fight hadn't changed very much throughout the years. Much like their predecessors, when Rapinoe, Alex Morgan, Hope Solo, Becky Sauerbrunn, and Carli Lloyd filed their EEOC complaint, they were using the success of a World Cup win to strengthen their hand against the federation.

That EEOC complaint, filed in March of 2016—after the team's World Cup win in Canada and prior to the 2016 Rio Olympics, opened with multiple points of evidence to the historical success of the women's national team: the three World Cup titles, four Olympic gold medals, other trophies in smaller international tournaments, and the team's No. 1 FIFA ranking. The five players on the complaint referenced the television rankings for the 2015 World Cup final and the attendance figures for the Victory Tour, as well as the income generated

100 Peterson, Annie. "History repeats: US women's soccer team still in wage fight," *Associated Press*, April 17, 2016. apnews.com/10df9310269c4d808e65637b7996a70e/history-repeats-us-womens-soccer-team-still-wage-fight

during the federation's 2016 fiscal year and projections for the 2017 fiscal year. All of these data points led them to one conclusion: despite their success, they were not being treated equally by US Soccer.

"Unfortunately, the WNT's on-field accomplishments and revenue generation have not resulted in us or our fellow players earning equal or better pay than MNT players," section V of the complaint read. "In fact, our compensation pales in comparison to that of the MNT players. This despite the fact that, as our employer, the Federation is bound by federal law to compensate us at least equally to the rate at which it compensates MNT players given that the women and men perform the same job duties; have jobs that require equal skill, effort and responsibilities; and perform our jobs under similar working conditions."[101]

The complaint was also filed after two key events that caused tensions to rise on both sides: a terrible playing surface selected for a friendly match in December 2015, followed by the federation suing the players association in early 2016 over their collective bargaining agreement's validity.

First: the playing surface, a decision made by US Soccer which nearly derailed Megan Rapinoe's soccer career.

The USWNT was set to play its first ever game in the state of Hawaii as part of the post-2015 World Cup

---

101   2016 EEOC complaint, PDF. http://big.assets.huffingtonpost .com/EEOCCharge.pdf

Victory Tour. In the end, the game would never be played. The team wrote its own version of what happened for *The Players' Tribune* to explain the decision-making process to the fans, many of whom were hoping to see the players in action for the very first time.

"On Friday at practice, we lost a teammate, Megan Rapinoe, to an ACL injury," the story explained. "Megan's injury took place while playing on a subpar training field. The grass on the training pitch itself was in bad shape. All along the pitch, sewer plates and plastic coverings were laying on the sidelines."[102]

Rapinoe never even made it to the stadium, which also proved to be unplayable. The team described the stadium's field conditions: rocks on the field and turf pulling up from the ground. The players were concerned the turf itself hadn't been replaced in years.

The players agreed: the stadium's surface was not fit to play on. The coaching staff also agreed. The federation was in charge of the final decision, but ultimately the game was called off.

The players shared their justification for their refusal in the story, as it went beyond their own health and safety, as important as those concerns were. Refusing to play on subpar surfaces meant avoiding future injuries, but was also a step for the overall protection of women's soccer players in general, not just for the national team.

102 "Equal Footing," *The Players' Tribune*, December 7, 2015. www.theplayerstribune.com/en-us/articles/uswnt-match-canceled -field-conditions

For too long, they accepted playing wherever the federation had asked them to, despite the risks. By demanding equal treatment to the men's national team, they'd get a shot at the same safety and protection the men earned from US Soccer.

This wasn't the first time the players tried to ensure they were playing on premium fields. They also fought against artificial surfaces earlier that same year, as the entirety of the 2015 World Cup in Canada was played on turf—essentially as a test run to see if it would ever be feasible for the men's World Cup. The players tried their best to stop the decision, though they ultimately failed in those efforts.

After the World Cup win, Rapinoe was asked if she changed her own opinion on turf, after playing on it for a month and still being successful. She still hated it.

"Honestly, I think it's even more crap now than I did before. I hated playing on it. And look, I get it … We don't have the ability to play on natural grass fields all the time. Sometimes it's not logistically or financially possible. But at the international level, to hold a major money-making global spectacle and to have to play on turf is ridiculous, in my opinion. The World Cup is hard enough on your body due to all the travel. To add extra wear and tear because of the turf isn't fair. I definitely felt it on my lower back and my ankles in particular," she wrote.[103]

---

103   Rapinoe, Megan. "Mailbag: Megan Rapinoe," *The Players' Tribune*, October 22, 2015. www.theplayerstribune.com/en-us/articles/megan-rapinoe-uswnt-qa-mailbag

Rapinoe understood that it had been too late to change FIFA's mind for the 2015 World Cup, but she expected better in the future. Beyond the simple demand of no World Cups ever on turf again—for men or women—Rapinoe thought that FIFA should also be the worldwide leader when it comes to such safety issues, and for equality between the men's and women's games. Who better to set the standard, after all?

As for her actual injury in December 2015, the ACL tear in her right knee could not have come at a tougher time, with the timing of the 2016 Olympics. As light-hearted as she was in the team's release about the injury, joking about playing FIFA 16, it was hard to ignore how avoidable her injury should have been.

Only two months later, US Soccer sued the women's national team players association over the validity of the collective bargaining agreement, operating under a memorandum of understanding between both sides. The players brought on Rich Nichols as a new executive director for the PA, and he immediately attempted to state that the existing CBA was not actively in effect for the national team.

The federation expressed regret in its statement that it had to take its own national team to court, but also made sure to remind the team and its fans that US Soccer was the international leader for support of women's soccer. It also promised to continue to work directly with the players to address concerns, but also to continue to grow and improve the game.

In June 2016, Judge Sharon Johnson Coleman decided in favor of US Soccer in US District Court in the lawsuit over the validity of the CBA and memorandum of understanding. The players were then held to the existing CBA, including no strike and no lockout provisions—removing one of their most powerful weapons, as shown by the 1995 and 2000 USWNT labor movements.

Between the unplayable turf field and Rapinoe's ACL tear in Hawaii, combined with the successful legal action from the federation, the five players tried to ratchet up the pressure on US Soccer the only way they could see—through the Equal Employment Opportunity Commission.

Winston & Strawn, the law firm that filed the action with the EEOC on behalf of the players, issued a press release that summed up the primary reasons for the decision to explore a new avenue outside of the collective bargaining process. Four of the five players are quoted, in a series that reads as a complete thought—first and foremost, that the players had been perhaps too patient with US Soccer, thinking that they would come to their senses and do the right thing by the WNT and pay them equally. Rapinoe's part pointed out that the players realized US Soccer would do no such thing however, setting up others to state that the team had no choice but to pursue an EEOC complaint, and that the team's performance backed up their requests for equal pay and treatment.

While the complaint was filed in March, by July, with the knowledge that a decision from the commission could take months, Rapinoe and the team expanded the fight to the public sphere as well. The players kicked off a new campaign via social media around the tag line "Equal Play, Equal Pay."

Only weeks away from the start of the 2016 Olympic tournament, Rapinoe sounded annoyed more than anything else when she spoke to the *New York Times* about the actions the players were having to take.

"We would prefer not to have to deal with this," she said. "But we're not going to shy away from it, either."[104]

Even with the EEOC complaint filed and the ongoing legal action between both sides, the players were still in negotiations with US Soccer over the next version of the CBA. Rapinoe, in the midst of a quick rehab turnaround from her ACL tear, expressed further frustrations with the progression of those talks.

She told the *New York Times* that summer that there was no movement on US Soccer's part, and she called out then-president of the federation, Sunil Gulati.

"It's quite frustrating to know that he's making comments that he wants to get a deal done, but he hasn't come to one meeting," Rapinoe said in 2016. "I've been to three meetings, flown six hours across the country and interrupted my rehab to come to New York, where he lives. And he can't come to one meeting."[105]

---

104   Das, Andrew. "US Women's Soccer Players Renew Their Fight for Equal Pay," The *New York Times*, July 7, 2016. www.nytimes. com/2016/07/08/sports/soccer/us-womens-soccer-players-renew -their-fight-for-equal-pay.html
105   Ibid.

Rapinoe's own role in the equal pay fight grew complicated, thanks in large part to her decision to kneel during the national anthem. While the issues were connected in her mind, because of her tenuous position with the federation and the coaching staff, she was essentially sidelined from being front and center on equal pay for months.

By 2017, the players and the federation finally managed a new collective bargaining agreement (thanks in part to another new leadership voice at the players association in executive director Becca Roux), with terms that would last five years, through the 2019 World Cup and 2020 Olympics and into 2021.

This edition of the CBA, which is still in effect, did not address or solve the problem of equal pay.

The new agreement included multiple wins for the players, however, even as the actual pay structure remained the same (and by its very nature, different than that of the US men's national team). Base salaries got a huge bump, the players association took back control of some marketing rights for the players, and there were new, additional provisions to help cover the National Women's Soccer League.

As important as the 2017 collective bargaining agreement was, it was still a compromise in many regards. There was still an expectation that both sides would operate in good faith; that because of US Soccer's commitment to women's soccer, they could perhaps be counted upon to further invest. Either way, the team never actually rescinded their complaint with the EEOC.

"I am incredibly proud of this team and the commitment we have shown through this entire process," Rapinoe said after its ratification. "While I think there is still much progress to be made for us and for women more broadly, I think the (Women's National Team Players Association) should be very proud of this deal and feel empowered moving forward."[106]

As the cycle progressed and the 2019 World Cup in France inched closer, even as the players were happy with the result of the most recent negotiations, they also never lost sight of their ultimate goal: equal pay from US Soccer.

In early February 2019, the Equal Employment Opportunity Commission finally issued a Right to Sue letter to the five players who initiated the complaint, which finally opened the pathway to legal proceedings for the team and proved that the players had exhausted all avenues of resolution, including mediation, through the commission.

On March 8—International Women's Day—twenty-eight players on the US women's national team filed suit against US Soccer in federal court over gender-based employment discrimination. In their complaint, the players and their legal team expressed their belief that US

---

106 Hays, Graham. "US Soccer, women's national team ratify new CBA," *ESPN*, April 5, 2017. www.espn.com/espnw/sports/story /_/id/19082314/us-soccer-women-national-team-ratify-new-cba

Soccer violated Title VII of the Civil Rights Act of 1964 and the Equal Pay Act of 1963.

While the concept of equal pay proved to be the most visible once again, and the easiest for most to grasp when trying to sum up the years of back-and-forth between the players and the federation, the lawsuit itself did address other issues, including "playing, training and travel conditions; promotion of their games; support and development for their games."

"I think it is much more about pay equity, I think obviously that's the hot button issue," Rapinoe said on Good Morning America in March 2019.[107] But as much as money was a primary focus, the players wanted to frame it in the context of equal investment and equal respect.

As Rapinoe said, "In order to have a fair and balanced conversation about compensation, we need to look at everything. We need to look at the way the youth teams are funded, we need to look at the way our staff—our coaching staff, our medical staff—is funded. We need to look at promotion and branding and marketing and sponsorship, all of that. Until we do, until we have equity and equality of the men's and women's team on both those sides, we can't really say, 'oh, the men make this and the women make this.' We don't feel like we're funded equally from top to bottom, and that's really what we're

---

107 "Soccer stars speak out on gender discrimination," *YouTube*, uploaded by ABC News, March 11, 2019. https://youtu.be /D1gCNUgpl2Q

fighting for, a holistic approach to both programs for the federation."[108]

As much as the lawsuit was driven by the specific demands of the current generation of players and a three-year journey from the EEOC complaint, that framing—equal pay is only possible via equal respect and equal investment—didn't just show that the players evolved their own thinking and understanding of their labor, but also put it in a larger societal context.

As Rapinoe pointed out, no one was out here trying to deny that the pay gap as a concept didn't exist. She also said that their equal pay fight was an example for the world at large, and that the team would serve as allies to underpaid women around the world.

Thanks to the players' willingness to get involved in the larger equal pay movement, they also earned support from Time's Up. Throughout the World Cup, Time's Up promoted the team with their social media channels, and some of the actresses most involved with the group—Eva Longoria, Uzo Aduba, Jessica Chastain, Jennifer Garner, and Natalie Portman—attended a send-off match in California.

By August, they made the partnership official, unveiled at the start of the Victory Tour and the team's return to California. The work was simple: both the players and the movement would help raise money for equal pay initiatives for women in the workplace.

---

108   Ibid.

(This would, by the summer of 2020, also result in a NWSL expansion team in Los Angeles thanks to the efforts of Natalie Portman and a massive, star-studded ownership group.)

The players also earned support via sponsors—including one of US Soccer's own. First, Luna Bar, the energy bar brand (primarily targeted at women buyers) owned by Clif Bars, stepped in and paid $31,250 to each player on the team to close the gap between bonuses paid out to the women and men. Then Secret donated $23,000 per player on the World Cup roster to the players' association. Secret, an official federation sponsor, also ran a full-page ad in the *New York Times* which directly referenced that relationship.

"As a partner," the ad reads, "we know the US Soccer Federation is an organization of considerable strength. It has the strength to be on the right side of history. ... We urge the US Soccer Federation to be a beacon of strength and end gender pay inequality once and for all, for all players."

Even after splashy donations and print ads, neither brand stopped its work behind the scenes, putting additional pressure on US Soccer.

The federation hoped to avoid any big labor movements from the women's national team with the five-year term of the 2017 collective bargaining agreement. Instead, they got a lawsuit, timed ahead of the 2019 World Cup that extended through the tournament and into 2020. And of course, the USWNT lived up to the pressure of the moment with their win in France, strengthening their support in the court of public opinion, earning equal pay chants across the stadiums of France and upon their return home.

In addition to the necessary legal filings, US Soccer primarily limited their responses in the public sphere to two open letters from President Carlos Cordeiro. The first was released shortly after the lawsuit was filed; the second was released after the 2019 World Cup.

"US Soccer has been and continues to be a champion for women's soccer in the United States and on the global stage," Cordeiro's first open letter began[109], before listing the specifics of the various investments the federation has made in women's soccer, as well as reminding his readers that the same team negotiated the 2017 collective bargaining agreement.

Even as he said that he—and the federation as a whole—were "surprised" by the players' complaint, he was also doing his best to understand where the lawsuit originated from, even as the original EEOC complaint approached its third birthday. He said that he was looking forward to more meetings where the players and US Soccer could more fully understand each other's objectives, though, by that point they were fairly clear for even the most casual observer. While Cordeiro was optimistic that the federation and players were on the

---

109   Cordeiro, Carlos. "Open Letter from US Soccer President Carlos Cordeiro," US Soccer, March 15, 2019. www.ussoccer.com/governance /board-of-directors/us-soccer-president-cindy-parlow-cone /open-letter-2019-wnt-lawsuit

same side, with shared goals for the growth of women's soccer, his pleasant tone in open letters eventually shifted to something resembling those USWNT vs. US Soccer battles of the 1990s and early 2000s.

This time, Cordeiro and the federation attached a fact sheet, stating that the women actually did, contrary to popular belief, earn more money than the men. He pointed out that instead of a battle in the media, the federation had instead spared no expense to prepare the national team for the World Cup. The list included charter flights, training facilities, additional staff, and promotion and marketing.

The fact sheet began with this stat: "Over the past decade, US Soccer has paid our Women's National Team more than our Men's National Team. From 2010 through 2018, US Soccer paid our women $34.1 million in salaries and game bonuses and we paid our men $26.4 million—not counting the significant additional value of various benefits that our women's players receive but which our men do not."[110]

The federation also pointed to the different pay structures, including the guaranteed salaries for the women including NWSL play, as well as the differences in FIFA prize money between the two teams. And as always, the federation used its historical investment in women's soccer—"Over several decades, US Soccer has invested many

---

110   Cordeiro, Carlos. "Open letter to our membership from US Soccer president Carlos Cordeiro," July 29, 2019. www.ussoccer.com /governance/board-of-directors/us-soccer-president-cindy-parlow -cone/open-letter-july-29-2019-finding-common-ground

millions of dollars in women's soccer—likely more than any other country—and we will continue to do so"[111]— as a shield.

After all, not much changed with the federation's strategy, even since those earliest clashes with its own players, including those in 1995 and 2000.

"It's so frustrating, and it's surprising. Now? Still? It's been so many years and we've had so much success and there have been so many changes," Michelle Akers said in 2016. "But the stance is a constant: 'Look, you guys are lucky to play. You guys should be grateful to play.'"[112]

The federation was constantly messaging its own investments as a worldwide leader in women's soccer to the players and to its membership and the public at large. The fact sheet was only the latest example of this line of reasoning; that previous investments absolved them from any attempt at equal pay between the women's and men's national teams.

At the same time, US Soccer also hired lobbyists specifically to discuss the federation's math when it came to the debate over equal pay with elected officials, particularly when it came to Democratic candidates for the presidency. The federation spent money on two lobbying firms, thanks to apparent concerns that the USWNT

---

111   Ibid.
112   Peterson, Annie. "History repeats: US women's soccer team still in wage fight," *Associated Press*, April 17, 2016. apnews.com /10df9310269c4d808e65637b7996a70e/history-repeats-us-womens -soccer-team-still-wage-fight

could come up as a talking point in a larger national conversation about equal pay, perhaps including mentions during one of the Democratic debates. While these concerns never came true, it was another wedge between US Soccer and its own players.

"I would like to be shocked, but I guess it is sort of in line with their behavior over all these years, and especially recently," Rapinoe said of the move to hire lobbyists. "From a bigger perspective, they're obviously spending revenue, sponsorship dollars, revenue created from little kids who are playing soccer, from everyone, they're spending that money on—in essence, this is probably a little dramatic, but in essence—trying to stop equality in the country."[113]

Rapinoe wasn't impressed by Cordeiro's open letters either, but was encouraged by the fact that the public mostly understood it did not address the primary accusations in the lawsuit, and the federation presented their math in a biased fashion—both on the fact sheet, and in the lobbyists' presentation, which featured most of the same numbers.

Simply, Rapinoe didn't understand any of it. "From a PR standpoint, even if you don't believe in it at all, (equal pay) might just be a good investment moving forward."

As 2019 turned to 2020, relations between the players and the federation didn't improve. As part of a procedural

---

113   Linehan, Meg. "'I don't understand it': Megan Rapinoe responds to US Soccer's lobbyist hires," *The Athletic*, August 12, 2019. theathletic.com/1133154/

court motion filed in February 2020, US Soccer argued that the women's national team did not perform equal work to the men's national team, relying on depositions from players including Rapinoe, Carli Lloyd, Alex Morgan, and others.

Players were asked if they could compete against their male counterparts, and if men had greater strength and skills than the women's national team.

By the next round of filings in March, US Soccer's attorneys leaned in on this argument, suggesting that because men had a biological advantage over women, plus greater responsibilities due to the relative competition levels in men's soccer, the federation did not need to pay the women the same amount.

Immediately after the filings became public, fans, sponsors, media, and players all reacted. Brands like Coca-Cola and Volkswagen—major sponsors of US Soccer—disavowed the arguments. Media pointed out that US Soccer's argument essentially invalidated the entire concept of women's sports. The players staged a protest during their final match of the 2020 SheBelieves Cup, as they wore their warm-up jerseys inside out. The US Soccer crest was hidden, but thanks to the embroidery used on the kits, the four stars for the team's four World Cup wins remained.

Less than a week later, US Soccer President Carlos Cordeiro resigned, leaving Vice President Cindy Parlow Cone, a former US women's national team player, to take his place.

Lawsuits, lobbyists, mediation, collective bargaining, whatever obstacles stand in the way of the US women's national team, Rapinoe and her fellow players have been ready for every challenge so far and continue to do the work. "We won't accept anything less than equal pay," she promised.[114]

The team also wanted more than just equal pay. Whatever the outcome of the lawsuit, Rapinoe and the team drew attention to historical inequalities faced by women's soccer in America. Equal investment and equal respect rounded out the team's list of demands, even as the concepts got lost in the shuffle of media coverage.

Setting aside the particulars of the US women's national team's battle with their own federation, it's also abundantly clear that for Rapinoe, her experience has awakened her to the larger societal movement that surrounds the team— and given her a specific calling for the rest of her life.

"I am going to fight for equal pay, every day," she said, a week after winning the World Cup. "For myself, for my team and for every single person out there. Man, woman, immigrant, US citizen, person of color, whatever it may be. Equal pay, as the great Serena Williams said, until I'm in my grave."[115]

114   @GMA, Tweet, August 15, 2019. twitter.com/GMA/status /1161978856250564608
115   @MeetThepress, Tweet, July 14, 2019. twitter.com /MeetThePress/status/1150407074960105472

CHAPTER SEVEN

You must do your part to change the world around you

"It's every single person's responsibility."

MEGAN RAPINOE'S LIFE CHANGED WELL before she scored in the 2019 World Cup final, but that moment ensured that when she returned to American soil, she'd be greeted by plenty of new fans, supporters, as well as a decent number of detractors. For every burst of furious applause for Rapinoe, and Rose Lavelle and the rest of the team, fans also chanted for equal pay for the US women's national team.

Upon the team's return from France, World Cup trophy in hand, the US national team once again were honored with a ticker-tape parade down the Canyon of Heroes in lower Manhattan. As thousands of fans and supporters once again lined Broadway, with office workers in the buildings above helping to fill the air with the contents of their shredders, there was a notable difference to the day of celebration in 2019 compared to the very same event after the 2015 World Cup win.

There were, of course, the chants for equal pay along the route. There were the signs supporting the players' campaign, the signs supporting individual players (particularly Rapinoe). But fans also responded to a call of action, issued in part by a sponsor.

"Won't stop watching," the signs read—a pledge to the players of the US national team, to follow them along to their respective teams in the National Women's Soccer League, part of a campaign designed by Budweiser. Rapinoe was featured prominently on a few versions of these signs; a photo of her playing for Reign FC in front of half-filled stands in Seattle featured prominently as a part of the print and media campaign.

For as much as the World Cup win inevitably turned into a launching pad about larger societal issues concerning the wage gap and respect for women, there was still the matter of using the platform of the tournament to help support the domestic league, to grow its visibility and reach, to boost attendance and television ratings that could help turn one summer's momentum into longer-lasting success.

Rapinoe and the rest of the USWNT knew this better than anyone, having watched the efforts following previous World Cups. The NWSL saw a few measures of success in 2015, but the league hoped for a wave that would lift the league. Instead, it was a bump that didn't carry over in 2016. A disconnect in messaging didn't help matters.

In 2019, Rapinoe tied the concept of supporting the team's fight for equal pay with the concept of supporting the league itself. By proving demand for all levels of women's soccer, it would in turn create larger investments.

"Fans can come to games, obviously national team games will be a hot ticket, but we have nine teams in the NWSL, you can go to your league games," Rapinoe told Rachel Maddow on MSNBC, on an episode that aired the evening before the parade. "You can buy players' jerseys, you can lend your support that way. You can tell your friends about it, you can become season ticket holders.

"I think in terms of that, that's the easiest way for fans to get involved."[116]

In 2015, fans asked some lingering questions about US players' dedication to the NWSL in the wake of that World Cup win—national team players are actually paid for their NWSL play by the US Soccer Federation, as part of the federation's ongoing support for the league, and also to remove one of the largest expenses for the NWSL while the league finds its footing. But some doubted how the players could expend extra effort to support the

116   @MSNBC, Tweet, July 9, 2019, twitter.com /MSNBC /status/1148778086164566017

league, when their paychecks were being signed by US Soccer.

In 2019, those questions were all but thrown out the window. Rapinoe wasn't the only one using her national platform to promote the NWSL. Alex Morgan name-checked the league during a speech at the ESPY Awards; the rest of the team took their cues from the team's captains.

Utah Royals FC head coach Laura Harvey, who coached Rapinoe for years in Seattle—and who also saw what worked and what didn't work for the NWSL following a World Cup up close both in 2015 and 2019—had plenty to say when it came to expectations that players like Rapinoe should promote the league.

"Megan Rapinoe's talking about us on Rachel Maddow. Alex Morgan's talking on the ESPYs," she said in July, after one of the first matches back after the conclusion of the 2019 World Cup. "Like how are we not all over it? How are we not? I don't care if we pay Megan Rapinoe to stand in front of people and say it. Pay her! Because she gets more exposure than anybody. Pay her. Don't care. If that's what it takes for exposure for this league, do it. Jump on it. It's not going to happen by itself. There's an expectation, I feel, that the US players should do it. Why should they?"[117]

For Harvey, she thought players were more willing in 2019 to speak about the NWSL because they were

<hr>

117 Linehan, Meg. "'It's our responsibility': Laura Harvey on the NWSL's need to do more to capitalize on the World Cup bump," *The Athletic*, July 18, 2019. theathletic.com/1083426/

convinced of the league's sustainability. The league, after all, is the third attempt at a professional women's soccer league in the United States. The 1999 World Cup wasn't enough to keep the first pro league, Women's United Soccer Association, running for more than three seasons. The second attempt, Women's Professional Soccer, fell apart thanks in part to a bad ownership group right as the US national team earned plenty of coverage at the 2011 World Cup.

That may have played a part in it, but for Rapinoe, her desire to promote the league actually comes from a desire to simply have a domestic league to play in.

"I don't think there's any obligation other than your own self-interest and interest in the league to do better, because we all play here and we want to play here," she said during an interview with *The Athletic* in August. "I think that the NWSL has been incredibly beneficial to the national team and the individual players that play in it."[118]

There have been lingering frustrations for Rapinoe on the league front: her club team, Reign FC, relocated from Seattle to Tacoma, Washington, in order to continue its own existence. There were many reasons for the move, thanks primarily to a lack of facilities that would meet the league's minimum standards in the Seattle area. But for Rapinoe, there are still questions about why the men's professional soccer team, the Seattle Sounders, can fill

---

118   Linehan, Meg. "'I got famous for all the things I am anyway': Megan Rapinoe on transforming from activist to icon," *The Athletic*, August 21, 2019. theathletic.com/1152922/

an NFL stadium for matches, but Reign FC never broke through in the same way. The talent was there, the results were there—especially for two seasons in a row when the Reign finished the NWSL's regular season in first place.

"Why does everyone love the Sounders so much?" she asked. "Do they just love soccer? Because if they love soccer, then they would have come to watch us play. We were basically undefeated for two years and had five of the top 20 players in the world. Everyone's like—" and here she put on a sarcastic, mocking voice—"'Oh, what are we gonna do?' And I'm like, 'I don't know!' We're doing everything we can. I'm not sure what else needs to be the selling point in the league. The quality is already there."[119]

Much like the fight on the national team side, in Rapinoe's eyes, there are the same underlying issues on the club side. A lack of equal investment, absolutely a lack of equal respect. The issue is more difficult when it comes to the NWSL though: for the national team, it's all through US Soccer. The NWSL and Major League Soccer, the men's professional league in the United States, are two completely different entities. There's no one organization to point to and say that the system is rigged; there are larger issues when it comes to women's sports at play here.

"Are we approaching the women's game in the exact same way, trying to maximize everything we can to make it as good as we can on both sides in the same way?" she asked. "Well, clearly not—historically, and even still

119 Ibid.

now. In the NWSL, I think the owners do care, it's just that they don't have enough money."[120]

Ultimately, solving those problems does not lie on Megan Rapinoe's shoulders, even as she's seen many of the challenges faced by two professional leagues. In December, Reign FC found a new investor in OL Groupe, the same ownership group of Olympique Lyonnais, a French club with men's and women's professional teams as well as an academy system. Rapinoe previously played for Lyon in 2013 and 2014.

There's still the work ahead for attendance numbers and increased season ticket and merchandise sales. Reign FC will have a stronger foundation to do that work in 2020 and beyond, thanks to the new owners and increased investment. It's part of the wheel that Rapinoe pointed to all of 2019: more money means better results.

The success of Reign FC and the NWSL as a whole is part of the entire movement, but it's crucial that Rapinoe didn't lose sight of it even in the face of success and the growth of her personal platform. She never thought that promoting the league was a huge ask for her, or some sort of albatross around her neck, because in fact it was one piece of the overall puzzle.

Back to New York City and the parade down the Canyon of Heroes: the flatbed trucks carrying the floats and

---

120   Ibid.

twenty-three overly excited and somewhat intoxicated national team players headed up Broadway to their final destination: City Hall. A jam-packed courtyard awaited the players, full of supporters and media and plenty of people who supported the team in some way or another. There were more signs; the chants for equal pay started long before the trucks arrived.

Thanks to the 2015 iteration, there was a general understanding of how the ceremony would go: speeches from New York politicians, the handing out of keys to the city, but more importantly, speeches from the president of US Soccer and the team's captains. There was, in essence, a showdown about to happen between the two sides. The players could absolutely be expected to not shy away from the issue of equal pay, especially with the amount of public support they enjoyed in general, not just on this one morning in New York City. But what would Carlos Cordeiro, the federation's president, say in the face of so much overwhelming support for the team?

"To our women's national team and the millions who support them, in recent months, you have raised your voices for equality," he said, this comment earning some cheers from the crowd, perhaps anticipating that this might be the moment where the fight could actually take a turn.

It wasn't the case. Instead, he pointed to the federation's investment in women's soccer, hitting many of the same talking points of his open letters. He targeted FIFA instead as well, hoping to find a common enemy. The crowd began to chant once more, so loudly that Cordeiro was forced to pause his speech.

The first part of the showdown was complete; Cordeiro made his play at walking the delicate line of not promising anything, while still pointing at potential reconciliation.

Rapinoe, from where she was seated on the stage, raised her hands as she clapped.

She was up next, walking to the podium without any prepared remarks, but two goals in mind: addressing Cordeiro and the federation face to face, and reaching beyond this one specific moment in time to make a larger call to action.

Rapinoe used humor to defuse some of the tension, joking about the reaction Cordeiro had just gotten from the crowd, then followed it up with a conciliatory attempt—not a concession—to affirm the federation's efforts so far. After all, there is no dispute on the facts of US Soccer's track record when it comes to women's soccer in comparison to other countries. The USWNT began the decade as the number-one ranked team in the world, and it ended the decade holding that exact same position on the rankings. That's not an accident.

Rapinoe took a risk: she backed Cordeiro in this speech, perhaps once again hoping for the best for a federation that had so far not rewarded her patience. But she had seen him every single day in France, backing the team, and for Rapinoe, that was a commitment that couldn't be overlooked.

In this speech, the first of many post–World Cup, Rapinoe used the team's support in the public sphere to position herself and the USWNT in a less threatening way—for many, women asking for more money will always be viewed as a threat to the status quo. She extended the benefit of the doubt to the federation and to Cordeiro himself, to affirm that everyone was coming to the table in good faith—to allow a path for both sides to move forward together to continue to grow the game.

But Rapinoe did not close this section of her speech without a reminder to the federation and a promise to the team's supporters. Rapinoe wasn't trying to play at being naive, just willing to open the door to more productive conversations between both sides.

As she said, "We look forward to holding those feet to the fire."

The first goal complete, Rapinoe moved onto her second: thinking bigger than just women's soccer, making the most of her platform to issue a call to action to everyone at City Hall, everyone watching on television or live streams, everyone who would later go on to read her words or watch clips of her speech—regardless of whether or not they agreed with her.

She issued a charge to everyone listening. "We have to be better," Rapinoe said. "We have to love more, hate less. We've got to listen more and talk less. We've got to know that this is everybody's responsibility, every single person here, every single person who is not here, every single person who doesn't want to be here, every single person who agrees and doesn't agree, it's our responsibility to make this world a better place."

She urged people to look to their own communities first, to come together and collaborate. She wanted everyone in that New York City audience, everyone watching on the Internet and TV to step up, to be better. She asked those watching and listening to look to her team, to view it as an example. She and her teammates shouldered great responsibility, she said, with a smile on their faces. It was only right for everyone watching to do the same.

Rapinoe tackled four of her biggest ideas in her approach and call to action—four lessons that have come from her experience both on and off the field.

First: assume personal responsibility for a collective goal. Rapinoe believes that there is a higher purpose in bettering the people around you, not just friends and family, but people who share the same community.

Second: talking is good, action is better, collective action is best. Listening is also a key driver here, which is necessary before action. The visibility element—talking, tweeting, writing, etc.—cannot be discounted, but it's only the first step of the process, and it cannot be done without listening to ensure other voices of the community are heard.

Third: the understanding that no one is perfect; there are no purity tests that need to be passed, just a desire to do better. Rapinoe stated many times over the span of years that she knows she's not perfect, especially when it comes to activism. Engaging with an open mind, the willingness to listen, the ability to course correct or step back, and perhaps the knowledge that the instinct to be defensive about previous thoughts or actions has to be put aside are all part of this lesson.

And finally: be bigger, but start by thinking smaller. Stepping up to do the work and assuming personal responsibility in a larger movement hits the first point, but Rapinoe also understands that not everyone is capable of leadership on a grand scale.

"You're someone who walks these streets every single day," she said. "You interact with your community every single day."

Thinking smaller isn't a failure of the call to collective action; in Rapinoe's mind, these all add up to a much larger movement.

And if there's a perfect example of how this call to action from New York City works in practice, it's the Burlington High School girls soccer team in Vermont.

The team earned plenty of headlines in October 2019, thanks to the events of a regular-season match-up against South Burlington. After scoring a goal to take the lead over their opponents, a few players ripped off their Burlington Seahorse jerseys to reveal shirts underneath that read "Equal Pay." The players were yellow carded for excessive celebrations; South Burlington scored a goal to force a 1–1 draw, and in the end, the story went viral for days across the country.

It didn't start at that particular match, however. One of the team's captains, Helen Worden, was in the stands at Stade de Lyon, listening to those equal pay chants after the US national team won the World Cup over the Netherlands in July. The second crucial event was another student, Maia Vota, actually traveled to New York City for the parade and City Hall celebration. She heard Rapinoe speak in person, asking the crowd to do what they could, to be bigger, to think about what they could do in their communities.

Vota went home to Burlington, and took those words to heart. First, Vota and the team thought up making equal pay t-shirts, but kept thinking bigger. Their ideas became an actual campaign after they found Change the Story, a local non-profit organization working to end the wage gap and further women's economic security in Vermont.

They designed equal pay jerseys, and started selling them locally, charging a little extra for men's cuts to drive home the point. Each shirt came with a tag that included facts about the wage gap, both locally and nationwide.

From call to action, to action itself. The Burlington Seahorses didn't stop after going viral either; a few brands stepped in to provide additional funds to help them out, and they still want to run clinics for youth players to try to pass the baton on to another generation, like the USWNT did for them.

When Rapinoe found out about everything accomplished by the girls from Burlington, she had a very simple reaction: "That's dope."

As excited as she was to see people inspired by her speech, it was also evidence that her four lessons—assuming personal responsibility, taking collective action, not worrying about being perfect, and embracing a smaller reach—served as practical instruction, that people desired to pitch in at every level. "I think just the power of the movement right now, that just proves it," she said in an interview in November. "Proves it all. People are here for it, they want it, it's something that's important to them."

And for Rapinoe, it was also proof she was on the right track in her own work. "I didn't know that the one who's helping to lead the charge was there that day," she said. "That's good. She heard the charge. That's exactly it, that is what I want to do."

Rapinoe never got the choice, as a female athlete, if she wanted to promote her own sport or not. She chose not to shy away from the responsibility to do more—not just for herself as a player, but for the professional league as a whole, for equal pay for her team, for what she considered her community. Every person had to do their part; hers was just a little bigger. She was ready to be a little louder to meet that challenge, to make that call to action.

The next generation heard Rapinoe's call, and more importantly, understood the reasoning behind it—that soccer might have been the platform but there's a much larger goal in mind.

"I think, ultimately, women's soccer needs to be about much more than how they're affecting young girls and our daughters and all that—there's so much more to it," Maia Vota said about her takeaways from the summer of the USWNT and how their fight for equal pay translates into a smaller scale. "Our big goal is, we want jerseys in as many hands of the people as possible so that people know about the wage gap.

"We've really tried to make sure we get this message out to men, specifically, and just really as diverse a group as possible, to get them in these jerseys and have them understand what's going on, because it's about much more than soccer."

CHAPTER EIGHT

Demand accountability from those with power

"Do anything. We have incredible power in this room."

AFTER WINNING THE WORLD CUP with the US national team, Megan Rapinoe still played some soccer throughout the close of 2019—but she also spent a lot of time talking. Whether in interviews or speeches, she defined her platform, examined her privilege, issued a call to action, and frequently, took advantage of the situation she was in to speak truth to power.

Rapinoe's never been afraid to call people or institutions out to their face, directly. For example, she answered every question about FIFA's lack of investment into the women's side of the game during the World Cup, including questions asked during FIFA's own official press conferences.

In New York City, she promised US Soccer President Carlos Cordeiro that the team would forge ahead if they didn't see results on the equal pay front. If invitations to negotiate in good faith didn't work, if the conciliatory efforts fell flat, she was prepared to use whatever methods it took to actually see results.

In Milan, after winning the FIFA Best Player of the Year award, Rapinoe was ready to do it again. But before Rapinoe took the stage, the president of FIFA, Gianni Infantino, took a few moments to address some of the systemic issues that FIFA and the global game encountered throughout the year.

Before he presented Lionel Messi with the men's player of the year award, Infantino said that racist behavior could not be deemed acceptable anymore—not exactly a radical position for 2019, but still notable for the fact he felt the need to say it.

"We have to say no to racism in whatever form," Infantino said. "No to racism in football, no to racism in society. But we don't have just to say it, we have to fight against it. We have to kick racism out once and for all—in Italy and in the rest of the world, out of football and out of society."

And before he presented Rapinoe with her award, he also promised increased investment into the women's game, including new tournaments such as a Club World Cup and Nations League. He also addressed stadium access for women in Iran, as activists fought for the right to watch matches in person despite being banned by their own government from doing so. In 2019, an Iranian fan named Sahar Khodayari (who went by the nickname of Blue Girl) died after setting herself on fire outside of a Tehran court, after being prosecuted for sneaking into a match dressed as a man.

Infantino promised that, "The world will have its eyes on Iran, and looking at women entering stadiums in Iran for football games."

So by the time Rapinoe made her way to the stage to accept her award, many of the topics she already planned to address had already been brought up by the most powerful man in the room—even though he never delved into specific action plans. Rapinoe admitted after the ceremony that she was a bit surprised at Infantino's comments, though pleasantly so. But she also knew it was the end result of the work that she and many others had done, to force FIFA's hand in being more active and involved to actually find solutions.

She was ready to continue that push—not just for Infantino, but for the rest of FIFA, for all of the famous male and female players, the coaches, the administrators in the room. She was ready to ask for everyone to actually act upon his words and his promises.

But she also wasn't about to let the opportunity slide for one quick crack about the sudden shift in attention for the women's game.

"As Gianni was saying, this was an incredible year for women's football," she said during the beginning of her speech. "For those of you who are just noticing that now, it's okay, you're a little late to the party but we'll forgive you. We're just getting started."

It was another reminder that Rapinoe has always been a master of humor, of knowing just how much edge to apply to her joke, to also help defuse her audience before she gets to the real meat of what she's about to say, the ask she was about to make.

She told the assembled crowd in Milan that every single person in that room had an opportunity, thanks in large part to their success on the field—and their financial success. Every person had a platform, and Rapinoe wanted them to use it and share it.

She believed that the sport could change the world for better, but only with intentional action.

In her speech, Rapinoe referenced two specific players when it came to international soccer's problems with racism. Raheem Sterling, who in December 2018 suffered racist abuse from the stands during an English Premier League match, then again in 2019 along with two teammates during an England match. Sterling used his own social media to point out the media's role in fueling both "racism and aggressive behavior," thanks to the difference in how they approach coverage for white players versus black players.[121]

Napoli's Kalidou Koulibaly became the face of trying to fight back against racism in the stands of Serie A,

---

121   @Sterling7, Instagram, December 9, 2018. www.instagram .com/p/BrKYvF3gH9e/?igshid=ir6sl8m1enxf

the top-flight men's professional league in Italy, after a match against Inter Milan. Milan supporters targeted him with monkey chants the entire match, and later, Koulibaly's own coach said that the game should have been suspended.

Much like Sterling and his conclusion that racist stands could not be divorced from racist media coverage, Italy's political climate was directly tied to the racism encountered by players in Serie A—prompting both Infantino and Rapinoe to address it.

But while Infantino issued a broad rejection of racism, Rapinoe demanded accountability from the players, the coaches, the administrators in the room—there were mechanisms to address racism, sexism, and other discrimination from the game, beyond platitudes. It's just that no one chose to do uncomfortable work. Rapinoe wanted to change that.

"You can't see the situation in Italy without removing it from its current political situation, with right-wing populists running the government," Piara Powar, executive director of Football Against Racism in Europe, said. "Every week, if not every day, you have a statement about immigration coming from the government which is always negative and always poses immigrants as problematic."[122]

---

122 Williams, Tom. "Kalidou Koulibaly: Napoli's Hero Fighting Racism in His Own Unique Way," *Bleacher Report*, January 25, 2019. bleacherreport.com/articles/2817575-kalidou-koulibaly-the-napoli -hero-fighting-racism-in-his-own-unique-way

Rapinoe also mentioned Collin Martin, an MLS player, the only out player in the league—and upon his announcement in June 2018, the only out male player across the five major leagues in America.

While there have been formal action plans in place from FIFA and anti-racism campaigns from leagues (Serie A actually launched one such campaign after Rapinoe's speech at The Best awards; the campaign posters included monkeys and were widely considered a terrible gaffe), actual results have lagged.

"So many times we say there is no place for racism in football, but nonetheless we still face challenges to tackle this problem in our sport, as we do in society. We will need the support of public authorities to help us identify and punish the culprits but we probably also need to think more broadly on what we can do to fix this," Infantino said after racist incidents took place in Bulgaria in a match against England.[123]

While he pointed to specific procedures to combat racist behavior, he admitted that they weren't enough, and organizations at all levels needed to go back to the drawing board. "We could not have imagined that so shortly thereafter we would again be having to think of how to combat this obnoxious disease that seems to be getting even worse in some parts of the world."

---

123 FIFA, "Statement following racist incidents in Bulgaria," October 15, 2019. www.fifa.com/who-we-are/news/statement -following-racist-incidents-in-bulgaria

For Rapinoe, all these issues were interconnected—racism, homophobia, sexism. But only a handful of names were speaking up, and all of them had experienced discrimination themselves. Where were the allies? Why were those with platforms waiting to share them, those with power so reticent to use it?

So the call to action for everyone in Teatro all Scala, the opera house in Milan that was hosting the awards ceremony: use the platform, use the sport itself, to figure out how they could help.

"Do something. Do anything." It wasn't exactly a major ask on Rapinoe's part—but still a necessary one. And while her fundamental message of calling people to find what actions they could take wouldn't change, over the course of the rest of the year, she would grow bolder as she called specific institutions and people out by name.

Rapinoe spun the idea of accountability in a different direction at another acceptance speech of 2019, for the *Sports Illustrated* Sportsperson of the Year at an event in New York City. She designed this speech specifically for the room of journalists and photographers and members of the media.

Rapinoe wanted to talk about the concept of witnessing. First, she introduced it in the realm of sports, of "witnessing greatness, witnessing a performance," tossing out names like Shaquille O'Neal and Serena Williams and Michael Jordan and LeBron James. She told a story about having *Sports Illustrated* delivered to her house and getting the magazine, only to rip a photograph of Michael Jordan out so she could pin it to the wall in her bedroom. She found the idea of her being celebrated by the same outlet to be surreal, even after winning back-to-back World Cups.

At the same time, she had this same concept of witnessing rolling around in her head for a very different reason, as she had just finished *Catch and Kill* by Ronan Farrow, a book that detailed Farrow's difficulties in reporting on Harvey Weinstein. The book clearly impacted her, and redefined what shape a journalistic platform could take, what stories it could be used to tell. Who might choose to tell those stories, or bury them completely? She revisited the concept of responsibility; in this case, not just Farrow's responsibility for the women he was writing about, but a responsibility for truth.

That truth—as important as her concept of what it meant to have a platform, it also required the element of truth for it to have power, for that power to be deserved.

"To bear witness, by definition, is to show that something exists or is true," she continued. "Think about that for a second. Show something exists or is true. As members, as a lot of you are, of the media, myself as a public figure, whatever that means, to have some sort of platform—this goes so far beyond any playing field or any story that we could write.

"And while we don't get to choose what it is that we witness, we are the gatekeepers of those stories. And we do get to decide how we bear witness to the world around us, and to the truth that we see."

At this point, Rapinoe paused from her actual speech to ask a series of questions to the room, filled to the brim with *Sports Illustrated* employees. First, she asked if it was true that she should be only the fourth woman deserving of the award. As soon as she asked, she dismissed the thought, which was met with extensive applause.

Serena Williams won the award in 2015, but before that, the last time women graced the cover was in 1999, after the US national team won the '99 World Cup. Rapinoe was only the fourth woman to ever earn the award solo, alongside Williams, track and field champion Mary Decker in 1983, and tennis star Chris Evert in 1976. The award has existed since the magazine's creation in 1954.

She continued, pointedly asking why *Sports Illustrated* featured so few diverse voices, particularly from people of color. The cheers were not as loud for round two. And she had one more, this time about the lack of women writers for the publication. In three questions, she called out not just who the people behind the magazine chose to celebrate, but the diversity of the very people who were making those decisions.

Rapinoe only had one final point for her audience, tying her success—in this case, less about on-field success and more about off-field—and this award to that act of witnessing, to that constant refrain about how people can be better.

"I think my success bears witness to not only the necessity of speaking truth to power, but just the power of truth," she said. "I invite, I encourage, I urge, I demand, I will hand-hold your ass to this. And whatever other way it needs to be said to you. But for all of us to think deeply about the way we bear witness to the world around us, in our communities, in our workplaces, in our work, in our relationships, and ultimately, in our shared experience—because that's really all this life is. 'Cause not only do I believe that we can be better, I believe that we together, we just are better."

Eventually, Rapinoe grew frustrated enough by the lack of a response to call people out by name—with three of the biggest names in men's soccer: Lionel Messi, Cristiano Ronaldo, and Zlatan Ibrahimovic—after winning the Ballon d'Or in early December. The award, presented by the weekly soccer magazine *France Football*, was only instituted in 2018 for the women, after being presented to men since 1956.

She asked for their help in Milan at the FIFA awards, but with their relative inaction on so many key issues regarding racism and sexism in the sport, she went one step further.

"I want to shout, 'Cristiano, Lionel, Zlatan, help me!'" Rapinoe told *France Football*, as part of an interview for the award (Rapinoe did not attend the ceremony in France; her original answers were translated into French for the article, then translated back).

"These big stars do not engage in anything when there are so many problems in men's football. Do they fear losing everything? They believe that, but it is not true. Who will erase Messi or Ronaldo from world football history for a statement against racism or sexism?" she asked.[124]

While Rapinoe was certainly on stronger footing than she was in 2016 after kneeling during the anthem, she still did not have the power of these three male players—even using social media metrics as a very inexact art of measuring reach, she has half a percent of their combined followers on Instagram.

Rapinoe publicly called out these three players, and asked for the bare minimum: a statement. For Messi, Ronaldo, and Ibrahimovic to use their words and their platform, even just once, to try and help bend the game in a more productive and equal direction.

Rapinoe never asked for detailed plans or guaranteed coverage of women's sports, just for people with power to do something, to start to figure out what action could

---

124   "'Do they fear losing?': Rapinoe urges Messi and Ronaldo to speak out on injustice," *The Guardian*, December 4, 2019. www.theguardian.com/football/2019/dec/04/megan-rapinoe-messi-ronaldo-zlatan-ibrahimovic-ballon-d-or

look like. To share the burden with players who experienced racism from the stands, and women and queer people who didn't feel like they were truly a part of the game. She asked people to witness this, rather than turning a blind eye.

After all, Rapinoe has always been ready to hold some feet to the fire.

CHAPTER NINE

Use your privilege to lift others up. Throw down your ladders.

"I think we can move on from losing alone to the belief in winning together."

MEGAN RAPINOE DEMANDED ACCOUNTABILITY OF others in her fight, but she did not forget to include accountability of herself and her own role in her work. That accountability doesn't necessarily include being perfectly on message all the time—Rapinoe knew that she would get some messaging wrong as she endlessly continued to learn—but instead she needed an awareness of why she was in those rooms with powerful people.

As organizations continued to present her with awards, she used one of those very speeches to point out some of the hypocrisy of the attention—that because she delivered the message, as a white woman, it became more palatable to the general public.

Most importantly, she worked to decenter herself as part of a larger movement, even as she made the most out of the attention, the awards, and the platform these two things provided her.

Accepting one of *Glamour Magazine's* Women of the Year awards, she opened with a comparison of her own 2019 compared to Colin Kaepernick—who still had not found a starting job as an NFL quarterback. For the first time, she also admitted that some of the attention was uncomfortable for her. For Rapinoe, there was no greater evidence that white supremacy existed than her onstage accepting an award as a white woman, while a black man was still effectively banned from his career. She thanked Kaepernick, knowing that she wouldn't have enjoyed this personal success without his direct example.

She returned once again to her call to do more—not just for others, but for herself as well. She reminded her audience that everyone is facing injustice of some kind. For her, it was the equal pay fight against the US Soccer Federation. But this speech was one of the first in which she did not just attempt to use her platform, but to examine how she earned it, and what larger forces might have been at play.

"It would be a slap in the face to Colin and to so many other faces," she said, "not to acknowledge (them), and for me personally to work relentlessly to dismantle that system that benefits some over the detriment of others—and frankly, is quite literally tearing us apart in this country."

Opposite to that system, in Rapinoe's mind, was the concept of abundance, of collective work and action. As she said, her mother taught her and her siblings that abundance was more than just sharing and kindness, it also included—simply—"giving a shit."

The system in place was built on scarcity, a culture Rapinoe found no interest in. Instead of alienation and loss, people could decide to win together. Rapinoe wanted to reimagine success, reimagine power so they were not personal wins, but instead contributed to a collective society of abundance.

She immediately applied those concepts in the next section of her speech—placing herself in a wider context, acknowledging everyone that contributed to her platform, promising to lift others up. She put herself in a spectrum of collective action, past and present and future.

She refused to stand on a platform alone, even as she gave her speech. Her list of names included Kaepernick, but also included the women of the Black Lives Matter movement, of the MeToo movement, of Time's Up. Her names included historical figures such as Harvey Milk, Gloria Steinem, and Audre Lorde, who had paved the way. And her list of names included victims of police brutality and violence, such as Sandra Bland and Trayvon Martin.

And again, she stressed that she was only up on the stage, holding an award and speaking to a captive audience, because she is white.

Acknowledging her whiteness wasn't a new activity for Rapinoe; she grappled with it since 2016 and the first time she kneeled during the anthem. But to suggest that she had won this award, had won other awards, and had been granted success and recognition thanks in part to her identity as a cis white woman (compared to Kaepernick, a black man) during a speech intended as a thank you? It wasn't exactly a traditional move but served as an effective reminder that she wasn't necessarily a leader, just able to be loud.

Rapinoe wasn't the only person being honored that night. Other women honored included young environmental activist Greta Thunberg and Lucia Allain, Erika Andiola, Mayra Jimenez, and Andrea Meza of Refugee and Immigrant Center for Education and Legal Services (RAICES). She knew they were already putting in the work.

As always, she wanted to share a message, for the people in the room, out in the audience, ones that were important enough to earn invites to an event such as an awards gala. She issued another reminder to everyone listening to share their platform, but this time, she had found visual language that gave life to her traditional ask: "Throw your ladders down, because it's our time."

That image of a ladder being thrown down, so more can climb up—that single image summed up her entire point, that there is room for everyone to have a voice, and to be heard.

"We're ready for this, and it needs to happen," she said. "This is such a pivotal moment for us. There is so much momentum, but we have to move forward and we have to be better."

Even as these speeches went viral and impacted additional people who weren't in the room, Rapinoe's influence and message have not just extended beyond the world of soccer but have directly impacted other women's sports and players who have also been fighting for equal respect, equal investment, and—while perhaps not equal—at the very least, better pay.

Meghan Duggan, who captained the US women's national hockey team to a gold medal during the 2018 Olympics, lived through a battle of her own with her sport's governing body. The players of the United States women's national hockey team boycotted a major international tournament for increased salaries and investment. She's also paid attention to Rapinoe's rise, for a number of reasons.

"We play these sports because we love them and we're super passionate," Duggan said. "Now, in this day and age, sports allow you to create a platform that you can use what you've done as an athlete to speak on other things. That's something I personally really want to be known for and I want to do. Not just win a gold medal and do nothing with it, but win a gold medal and make change where change needs to be made. And I think Megan is an awesome person to idolize in that sense."

Duggan also found Rapinoe's ladder metaphor to be a direct invitation into further action that she herself could take.

"I think she's a leader for all of us, and I learn something from her every single day about who I want to be and what I want to do and how I can be of service," she said. "We're all here to serve others and to speak out against any injustices."

Rapinoe's message goes beyond just how it might apply to women in sport. She pointed to Rapinoe's role within the LGBTQ community, the work being done with Time's Up, and how she has influenced women in other industries. Duggan thought Rapinoe was "empowering people," period.

As inspiring and empowering as others might find Rapinoe's message, it takes a certain level of courage to follow the instruction to throw down a ladder—it implies your own voice will be weakened, or perhaps not heard at all.

That's the power of using your privilege, as shown by Rapinoe. She did not lose her voice. She added a chorus, which in turn helped her be louder and ask for more. By throwing down her ladders, and highlighting the work and commitments of others, she didn't lose her platform, she grew it.

CHAPTER TEN

Grant recognition to those who paved the way, and let them help show you the way forward

"I'm not gonna stand there and pretend like I just did this all by myself."

IN NOVEMBER 2019, MEGAN RAPINOE spoke at an event hosted by Luna at the company's headquarters with Clif Bar in California. The brand had added Rapinoe to their list of sponsored athletes, but they had something special planned for this visit—they brought in Gloria Steinem to ask the questions.

The company had already staked its claim in the space for equal pay, and not just in women's soccer—though they had arguably made one of the biggest moves ahead of the 2019 World Cup. On Equal Pay Day, April 2, 2019, Luna had committed to paying each member of the United States national team an additional $31,250 directly—the exact difference of the bonus paid to the men's team for making a World Cup roster.

"Many brands raising awareness for equal pay use the USWNT's fight as an example, but don't go the extra step to offer a solution to the problem," the team's players association director, Becca Roux, said in April via a Clif Bar press release.[125] "Luna Bar has a long history of supporting women's equality and is truly walking the walk by maximizing the amount of money going directly to the players and intentionally closing one of their pay gaps."

Luna had also put on a number of other events and panels—including one during the World Cup at the Eiffel Tower in Paris—inviting athletes across multiple women's sports to speak about equal pay and other issues. For potential "Belief-Driven Buyers," Luna was all in their values as a company, and had jumped in headfirst on putting those values directly into action.

The panel gave Rapinoe an opportunity to put so much of her life and her activism in the same

125 Press release, "LUNA® Bar Moves US Women's National Soccer Team One Step Closer to Equal Pay," April 2, 2019. www.businesswire.com/news/home/20190401005973/en/LUNA®-Bar-Moves-US-Women's-National-Soccer

conversation—where choosing to play soccer as a child was tied to her identity as an adult as both an athlete and a member of the United States national team; where equal pay was tied to media representation; where what she had experienced directly could be used for others to learn from. And she had a cheerleader and admirer across the stage from her in Steinem, who had also lived through her own versions of many of these same battles.

This wasn't the first time Rapinoe had met her—at the start of their panel, Steinem said that after Rapinoe had visited her home in New York City for an evening of conversation, all of her friends were trying to put a memorial plaque on the spot Rapinoe had occupied on her sofa.

"We have your address now," Rapinoe joked.

One of the things they had discussed while sitting on the sofa in Steinem's place had obviously been equal pay, and Steinem used that earlier conversation as a launching pad for their public discussion, especially around equal pay.

"The whole question of equal pay should be viewed as economic stimulus," Steinem said. She said that economic stimulus was traditionally framed in other ways, such as the stock market, but "actually the biggest stimulus would put something like 400 billion dollars more into this economy, would be equal pay by race and sex."

The biggest challenge to actually having that conversation, both Steinem and Rapinoe agreed on. "Women's issues are viewed as over here and not part of everything,"

Steinem said. For Rapinoe, the separation of "women's issues" didn't make sense, simply because men were connected to women in multiple ways.

Steinem then tied this disconnect to the concept of the patriarchy, and said that women were still gradually finding ways to escape the various methods of control of women's bodies, and that society was "gradually changing gender, which is also invented gender roles." Here, she said, was where Rapinoe was tied to a "long, deep revolution and evolution."

To Steinem, Rapinoe and the US national team, women's sports in general, were crucial, because they were "the one place where girls and women see that our bodies are not ornaments, they're instruments."

Rapinoe had found her own self-confidence in part thanks to sports, had found a safe space in that world, but also pointed out that she had become an adult in the ecosystem of the national team—surrounded by women of all ages as her teammates.

"It became normal for us to view our bodies as instruments and not ornaments," she said.

There was also power in the team. She wasn't isolated for wanting to play soccer, especially as an adult.

"I have always been surrounded by these women who use their bodies in their particular way, who use their voices in a particular way," Rapinoe said. "We aren't really interested or even trying to reach anybody else's standards. It's all about what the group is doing, and I think we empower each other and give each other confidence in that way. So it's almost kind of a group outside of this idea of our bodies being an ornament, or us having to look good for one thing or use our bodies for one thing, because we were always focused on getting the most out of it that we absolutely could in this particular field."

Rapinoe directly tied that environment to the team's decisions to fight for equality, how public reaction and even backlash against their public image has only strengthened their position.

"We kind of get into the world and people are like, 'Whoa, crazy! What are they doing? Why are they acting like that?'" That response and some of the larger societal biases, Rapinoe said, have creeped into their relationship with US Soccer.

She described the first time she went through collective bargaining with the federation in her career, early into her time with the national team. " I had no idea what that meant at all. Before that I was like, this paycheck is awesome, it just keeps coming every month, this is great," she said. But she also didn't understand the reason for the amounts on the paychecks, the bonuses, all of the factors that were affecting what the team was being paid.

While "the condescending tone with which [US Soccer] always speaks" hadn't changed over the course of Rapinoe's career, the players' reaction had. As she joked, "now we're like, 'helllll no, we're good, see you later.'"

But Rapinoe saw first-hand from her own viewpoint at the table, from the team's perspective, how the federation "always try to keep us down in the market, where women's soccer was growing, and growing, and growing every year." As the team became more popular after the 2011 World Cup, then the 2015 and 2019 wins, the federation's stance on "market realities" remained unchanged.

"I disagree, and I actually know that for a fact because we also have the luxury of going outside of the team and we have our personal brands and we have our personal sponsorships and our appearances that we get paid for, and it's like, it's really not adding up," Rapinoe said. "I think that they need a market reality summary on what's happening."

But Rapinoe hadn't walked into the room with all of this knowledge years ago; she called it an "education for the last 14 or 15 years." There were other factors as well, for her and for each generation of the team: insecurity about your roster spot, a lack of knowledge about gender discrimination.

But that education has meant she's now in a stronger space to spin what she's learned into lessons for others, not just for the general public at an event, but even within the national team itself.

For Rapinoe, there's one simple solution: talking about money openly, in as much detail as possible. She said the national team tries to do it internally as much as they possibly can.

"Talking about it all the time and helping to not only break the taboo, but also start to break some of the stereotypes and the lies and the sort of misdirection and confusion that happens with it, I think is really important," she said.

She and the other veterans try to educate younger players on the differences in the salary structures, why the bonuses between the men's national team are different than the women's national team. It's why the message around the equal pay lawsuit doesn't end with equal pay, but equal respect and investment.

"It's not just that our bonuses are different, it's that we're never gonna have the opportunity to even get on the same level if all of the investment isn't the same, the investment in our medical, our travel, our coaching staff, and marketing, the sponsorships, the branding, the ticket sales, I mean like everything that goes into it," Rapinoe said. It's why they try to avoid comparing TV numbers or ticket sales. "It's a whole business that has many different levels and dynamics to it. … Without everything else being equal, we can't even get to the conversation about compensation."

Transparency has been a key for Rapinoe, a personal responsibility.

"I want everyone to know exactly what I'm making. I don't see any reason to hide that because it only hurts everybody else," she said. She told a story of sharing the details of sponsorship agreement with a teammate, who had the exact same deal with the same brand. That teammate was making far less, and was able to renegotiate after talking with Rapinoe.

"It's not that everybody needs to make the same amount," Rapinoe said, "but we can start to discern what is fair and where we sort of land in the market with all of these things." Holding sponsors accountable, holding the federation accountable; these were both important goals for Rapinoe, but neither worked without actually sharing the information with her peers. "Clearly, it's being hidden for a reason."

Rapinoe also stressed transparency on other fronts—tying in all of her success to her identity, reinforcing the points she had made when she accepted the award from *Glamour Magazine*. She said again, that she would not be in this position without the actions and belief of Colin Kaepernick.

She hit the exact same points again. "We have a system that favors some people over the other," she began, pointing to Kaepernick's lack of offers from NFL teams. At the same time, while Rapinoe's career had been in danger for a time after kneeling, she was enjoying "unprecedented personal success."

That personal reward had one key factor for her still. "I think that my whiteness and white privilege and all that has so much to do with that, so I am under no misconception that I'm up here, yes, but there are a million other people doing the exact same thing and for them, they're the reason that I'm here, and they don't always get the opportunity to be there, to get the same opportunities that I've gotten."

While Rapinoe had been asked about advice for white women like herself, she expanded her advice to "anyone in a position of power, privilege, or influence." That advice was simply to be transparent while using that power, privilege, and influence, as she herself was trying to do.

"I'm not gonna shy away from this platform just because I had a head-start in getting it, but I'm sure as hell gonna make sure that while I'm on it, other people are gonna be on it with me. I'm not gonna stand there and pretend like I just did this all this by myself, I absolutely didn't."

She felt a responsibility to use the platform, to be loud, but she also did not want it to only be hers—in fact, her goal was to ultimately push herself farther back in the larger picture, to "let all the other people who I feel like really deserve to be out in the front be there, and until those people are up here and have the same opportunities and we can live in a much more equitable and equal place then it's my job to use whatever power and influence that I have to dismantle the system really that's benefiting me at the expense of others."

Thanks to the event's selection of Steinem as moderator, it also gave Rapinoe a chance to frame her own role in that larger front on a timeline—with Steinem and other activists who came before, and who might step in after.

"I feel like I honor what has come before by moving past those fights and fighting different things. It's like, if I'm still just lounging in the same place that someone was already at, that's pretty disrespectful and kind of lazy," she said.

One of the things that was talked about the most on the US national team was fighting the equal pay fight, so no one else would ever have to tackle it again—so others might use it as an example in other countries. Even the way the team tries to pass on the lessons to its rookies and younger players, to ensure that the movement carries on, is part of this work.

That's not to say the work doesn't frustrate her at times. She said that a good rant never hurt, particularly one with a few extra curse words thrown in. Having friends to be able to rant to, in an attempt to prevent cynicism, was important to her.

"I just cannot believe we're still dealing with this, I can't believe some of the things that people say and some of the arguments people make, it's outrageous," she said. "But also I see the world changing around me all the time. I see the progress that's being made through my career and certainly in this moment."

Having nine-year-olds ask about equal pay was a reward for her, for the work. But it also kept her going, especially since she understood that there was a ceiling to what she personally could achieve. "That kind of keeps me like really energized and motivated. You kind of have this goal that's unattainable, that you're probably, unfortunately, never gonna reach, but you always have that something to fight for."

Rapinoe was also asked about advice for men, in particular, when it came to equal pay. She didn't stray far from the messaging she had previously given to the men in the world of FIFA, but did note how important it was for men to step in when they felt something crossed a line—without needing to hear it from a woman first.

"Do something, do anything, do it all. Do something, talk about it, ask, lend your voice, show up in those spaces," she said. She mentioned that her USWNT teammate Crystal Dunn was always good about reminding her about the concept of collecting and correcting your own people, which in this particular situation, meant for men: "your guy friends, like with locker room talk, or like your family members or whatever it is, if there's some sort of offhand comment that you know is wrong, it's a difficult thing to do to collect and correct your own friends, and maybe they're saying something that doesn't really affect you personally, but you know it's not right, they wouldn't say it in certain settings, to always be bold and standing up in those moments. Those are things I think that really start to affect change is, the people we interact with every day, our friends, our family, our communities, and that sort of ripples out from there."

Steinem backed her up on this front—pointing again to Ronan Farrow as an influence, though in this case, that "because he is a man, he is taken with more seriousness" over the actual accusers of Harvey Weinstein.

Rapinoe bounced off of that point, saying that until a man is as upset as a woman would be by a sexist comment, or a white person is as offended by a racist comment as a person of color would be, change would be slow, at best.

"If we're all apathetic about it, then it's not gonna hit home, and it's not gonna make people change and it's not gonna bring it right to the forefront. So I don't know if that's a shift in perspective or a deeper sense of empathy or what, but until we're all affected by these things that really are truly disgusting, then it's not gonna change."

Rapinoe doesn't frequently talk about her fears, but did open up on this front as well. While she had shared her fear, to some extent, following kneeling for the anthem and how it could impact her career—not just from a sponsorship standpoint, but in regards to the national team—that decision has stuck with her, and perhaps not in the way that most might expect.

"Am I doing enough, am I doing it in the right way? Am I—" she said, pausing for a moment, "yeah, am I doing enough?"

Rapinoe had spoken about the power of a platform for months, but even she was wondering if she could be doing more, how much more she could put on herself.

"Like I know that I'm doing things, but I think sometimes balancing all the schedules and everything and talking about all these things, is talking just enough? I think that's something that I struggle with a little bit," she said.

As for the decision to kneel, she still had doubts on if it was truly enough, if by following US Soccer's bylaws she had put her own self-interest first.

"I knelt for a couple of games, and then was off a number of rosters really and I felt like they were trying to push me out. Of course they won't say that, but I was like, 'hmmm, 1+1 is 2, here we are,' but the federation made the rule to, you're not allowed to kneel or whatever. And I stopped kneeling. And I still, even with that, struggle a little bit. Because it was sort of protecting my self-interest in a way, I don't want to stop playing, I don't want to be out of a job or boycotted like Colin was."

So again, Rapinoe questioned herself: "Am I doing the right things? Am I saying the right things? Am I representing everything in the way that is best?"

Rapinoe said she tried to be educated, she tried to make sure she was doing things the right way. The fact that she had doubts isn't concerning, it's human. Back in France, she had acknowledged that she wasn't perfect, that others might disagree with her methods. Her willingness to learn on the fly, to release herself from the idea that she had to be perfect—even as it scared her and made her question itself—is also the exact same thing that made her effectively use her platform, simply because she was in fact willing to use it.

"Especially being a sort of famous-ish person in some kind of way, it is really important to speak up and to say things," she said, while still acknowledging for her that it was easy. She had access to media, she had access to events just like this. This very event was a part of her privilege.

"Is there other work that I could be doing that maybe is a little bit more of grind, or less in my self-interest, that is harder, that I should be doing? Or is like, or is this enough right now?" she asked, even perhaps looking to Steinem for some sort of affirmation.

"There's always like a million things, like, I'm sure you feel this, there's a million things you could be doing all the time, I mean you'll never be able to do enough, obviously until we have a perfect society which we probably never will have, but what is enough of making sure you're doing the right thing?"

Steinem simply reminded Rapinoe that her own soccer career had some lessons for her, that could help her solve the case of the "should" she had picked up ("What should we do, as opposed to doing whatever we can right now").

"Sports is the great teacher of that," Steinem said, "to be in the moment, to do what you love. That tells you what you're meant to do, and not to... you know you can't live in the future as it happens with all five senses, you can only live in the present with all five senses. So, you know, trust your instinct."

It's hard to predict what would have happened had Rapinoe continued to kneel after the US bylaw was put into place—would her career have followed Kaepernick's? Would she have shifted entirely into activism, would it have affected her NWSL career as well (especially considering the fact that US Soccer pays her NWSL salary)? Would her platform be as large as it became, thanks to the 2019 World Cup? It's hard to imagine it would be.

Steinem didn't dig into any of these ideas, but she did think that Rapinoe was deeply important for the world when it came to her visibility. Steinem told a story about when she had first moved to New York City. She was on 57th Street, and she saw another woman walking by across the street, in a raincoat, a cowboy hat, and cowboy boots.

"She was not carrying a purse—somehow that was very important to me—she was not carrying a purse, Nancy Drew also didn't carry a purse, anyway," Steinem said. "She was striding along and she looked free. And I thought, 'That is the first free woman I have ever seen in my life.' And I have never, never forgotten that."

As formative as that moment was for Steinem, looking at Rapinoe, looking at the United States women's national team as a whole, meant more. "Truly truly truly incredible, and I thank you so, so much for being an example. It really—nothing on earth is more important, nothing, nothing, nothing. Are you embarrassed by now?"

Rapinoe was embarrassed, but it's easy to understand how Steinem made the leap that she did, from one woman walking along 57th Street in New York City with no purse, wearing what she wanted, to Megan Rapinoe and the women of the national team, whose bodies were instruments instead of ornaments—to Rapinoe's pose, daring both an invitation and repudiation, the way she and the team took up space and challenged the status quo. That they were willing to ask for what was equal, in fact, that they were willing to ask for more, what they deserved.

CHAPTER ELEVEN

Don't listen when people tell you to stay in your lane

"I stand for honesty and for truth."

"Stick to sports."

It's a common refrain—as if sports can be completely divorced from society, as if politics do not directly impact sports, as if athletes should not be allowed to share their own personal beliefs and political thoughts.

Megan Rapinoe, and indeed, the entirety of the US national team, tossed the entire concept aside for years. People listened when they spoke, after all. Some rejected the idea of turning to a soccer player for political insight, but plenty more saw themselves in Rapinoe—and saw a new notion of American excellence. She represented America on the world stage, but also in a more conceptual, progressive fashion as well.

For Rapinoe, the willingness to ignore the "stick to sports" edict so could be traced back to the roots in her coming out in 2012, and her kneeling during the anthem in 2016, but no one could have fully anticipated the events that took place during the summer of 2019 and through the World Cup.

But even before the start of the tournament, Rapinoe and the rest of the players, the media, fans, the sports world in general, began grappling with the larger ideas of what it means to represent your country—how someone like Rapinoe could pull on the red, white, and blue, with a crest representing the United States of America directly over her heart, at this particular moment in time. That even as governments at every level across America sought to restrict women's reproductive rights, even as the team continued to fight for equal pay against their own federation, how to hold that at the same time as their roles as athletes on the largest platform in the sport.

In a cover story for *Time Magazine*, fellow co-captain Alex Morgan also said she would personally decline a trip to the White House, angered in particular by the current administration's immigration policies.

She also said she didn't particularly mind if that rubbed some people the wrong way.

"We don't have to be put in this little box," Morgan said. "There's the narrative that's been said hundreds of times about any sort of athlete who's spoken out polit-ically. 'Stick to sports.' We're much more than that, O.K.?"[126]

At the team's official media day, which took place in New York City at Twitter's headquarters, Morgan—and a handful of her teammates—weren't shy about engaging in political conversation, even with the tournament only a matter of a couple of weeks away at that point. At the same time, Morgan also stressed that these individual concerns, as important as they are, also needed to be bal-anced with the work the team was actually being paid to do: promote their campaign to win back-to-back World Cups.

"Right now, all eyes are on us," Morgan said at media day. "I think the tricky part is us wanting to stay focused on the World Cup, and what we're here to do. Obviously, there are a lot of distractions, but there are also a lot of more important issues that are bigger than soccer in the world today."

At that same event, defender Becky Sauerbrunn said while the team had to win in order to be invited, the gen-eral consensus of the team followed Alex Morgan's (and Rapinoe's). There was little interest in a visit to Trump's White House, though Sauerbrunn said the group would evaluate as a whole if a formal invitation did come.

---

126   Gregory, Sean. "'You Have to Take a Stand.' Soccer Phenom Alex Morgan Wants the Respect—and Money—Female Players Deserve," *Time Magazine*, May 23, 2019. time.com/5594356 /alex-morgan-world-cup/

So by the time Megan Rapinoe stepped into the room for her session with the media—in fact, the only player to get a solo media access time the entire day—she was swarmed with reporters who were very ready to stray from the very topic they were there to cover: the World Cup. And Rapinoe, as always, was ready to speak on these topics.

One of the things she stressed early was that the national team built solidarity with other movements, and these conversations were flowing in both directions.

"Anything from the (USA) hockey players (who successfully boycotted against their own governing body in a labor dispute) to us to #MeToo and Time's Up, all of it is sort of part of the same thing," she said. "And even beyond that, you know, Black Lives Matter and immigrant groups, all of it. Everything sort of plays off each other, and it's obviously in a swell right now, which is exciting."

She was also ready to dig into the specifics of women's reproductive rights, a hot topic at media day after Georgia, Alabama, and Missouri all pushed anti-abortion bills through at the state level during the month of May.

"Those people are going to do everything they can to keep all the power they have for as long as they possibly can," Rapinoe said of Republican legislators. "Maybe they feel like, you know it is that moment where it's kind of a tipping point—I don't want to say slipping away, because it's not their power to have, but things are becoming more equal for everyone, and I guess people are uncomfortable with that because they're selfish."

So even before the World Cup started, Rapinoe and Morgan especially, but to some extent a majority of the US national team, already shared some personal thoughts on how their platform interacted with the larger political direction of the country; and the equal pay lawsuit filed on International Women's Day was certainly a political act in and of itself.

(Rapinoe talked politics a lot after 2016, but there was one reference she made to Trump before his election. In a mailbag for *The Players' Tribune*, she was asked to play word association with a number of names, including Abby Wambach—"Tall"—and Donald Trump—"Jerk but funny."[127] Obviously, after 2016, her opinion changed considerably.)

So it wasn't exactly surprising that these issues would carry over to the tournament itself, even as FIFA and US Soccer did try to keep the focus on the games and players. They failed in those efforts.

The funny thing was, the video featuring Megan Rapinoe that went viral during the World Cup—the one that didn't actually even feature her playing in a World Cup,

127 Rapinoe, Megan. "Mailbag: Megan Rapinoe," *The Players' Tribune*, October 22, 2015. www.theplayerstribune.com/en-us /articles/megan-rapinoe-uswnt-qa-mailbag

or even on the field in any way—was actually filmed months before. During a photoshoot for Eight by *Eight Magazine*, an interviewer asked her about her and the rest of the US national team going to the White House if they won again during the summer of 2019.

Rapinoe scoffed, in the middle of suiting up in the team's new jersey for a photoshoot.

"I'm not going to the fucking White House,"[128] she replied, before expressing her doubts about if the team would even be invited by the building's current tenant.

It also wasn't even the first time Rapinoe stated on the record that she had no interest in going to the White House. In an interview published in May 2019 with *Sports Illustrated*, she said the exact same thing—only minus the cursing.

"Absolutely not," she told Jenny Vrentas on if she would even consider going to DC.[129]

"I am not going to fake it, hobnob with the president, who is clearly against so many of the things that I am (for) and so many of the things that I actually am," Rapinoe said in the interview, one that was also featured in the print magazine right before the start of the tournament in early June.

---

128   @8by8mag, Tweet, "'I'm not going to the fucking White House.'- @mPinoe" June 25, 2019. twitter.com/8by8mag/status /1143595809910530048

129   Vrentas, Jenny. "Megan Rapinoe Will Be Heard," *Sports Illustrated*, May 29, 2019. www.si.com/soccer/2019/05/29 /megan-rapinoe-usa-womens-world-cup-uswnt-voice

For a person obsessed with sharing her platform for good, interacting with the current president and extending the team's platform to him was the opposite of what she wanted to do.

Despite already having gone on the record, despite not being the only player who said she would skip a White House visit, despite the fact that the video was actually months old, it all came down to when the video was actually released. The video, a perfect bite-sized clip, dropped on June 25, 2019—the day after the United States defeated Spain in the round of 16, setting up the quarterfinal against host nation France in Paris on the 28th. It was the match of the tournament; Rapinoe herself wished for a spectacle and "shit-show" in the mixed zone after the first win of the knock-out round.

Political websites tried to stir up some new conflict around Rapinoe, particularly when it came to Donald Trump, already in the tournament. DC website *The Hill* started out their limited World Cup coverage at the start of the tournament with an article about how Rapinoe refused to sing with the anthem (a refusal she already explained on the record).

On June 24, the day before the video dropped, *The Hill* published an "exclusive interview" with Donald Trump—one that essentially boiled down to a couple of answers on both Rapinoe and the USWNT's fight for equal pay.

On Rapinoe's right to protest in a US kit, Trump told *The Hill* he did not feel it was appropriate. He also said that he "love(s) to watch women's soccer," and that the team was talented.[130]

On the matter of equal pay, he was less certain—and told *The Hill* that he had not taken a position on it. "I think a lot of it also has to do with the economics," Trump said. "I mean who draws more, where is the money coming in. I know that when you have the great stars like (Portugal's Cristiano) Ronaldo and some of these stars … that get paid a lot of money, but they draw hundreds of thousands of people."[131]

Of course, a day later after the video dropped, Trump cut out the interview process and took directly to Twitter to let Rapinoe know directly what he thought of the video, and her politics.

"I am a big fan of the American Team, and Women's Soccer, but Megan should WIN first before she TALKS! Finish the job! We haven't yet invited Megan or the team, but I am now inviting the TEAM, win or lose. Megan should never disrespect our Country, the White House, or our Flag, especially since so much has been done for her & the team. Be proud of the Flag that you wear. The USA is doing GREAT!"[132]

---

130 Fabian, Jordan and Saagar Enjeti. "EXCLUSIVE: Trump says it's not appropriate for Megan Rapinoe to protest during national anthem," *The Hill*, June 24, 2019. thehill.com/homenews /administration/450135-exclusive-trump-says-its-not-appropriate-for -megan-rapinoe-to-protest

131 Ibid.

132 @realDonaldTrump, Tweets, June 26, 2019. twitter.com /realDonaldTrump/status/1143892326286266368 and twitter.com /realDonaldTrump/status/1143892328236687361

The interaction between a player and president was unlike anything that had ever happened for the US national team—and for US Soccer, a national governing body that has particularly looked to the federal government (including Trump) for support. Mix the pressure cooker of the most important international soccer tournament, then add on a public feud with the President. It was distinctly uncharted territory for everyone—the players, the administrative staff, the media, the fans.

Rapinoe didn't have to stand alone, however. Ali Krieger was the first player to publicly voice her support for Rapinoe.

"In regards to the 'President's' tweet today, I know women who you cannot control or grope anger you, but I stand by (Megan Rapinoe) and will sit this one out as well," she tweeted. "I don't support this administration nor their fight against LGBTQ+ citizens, immigrants & our most vulnerable."[133]

With the increased time in between matches thanks to the tournament's format, the story had days to grow legs—and it certainly wasn't just limited to the sports reporters on hand in France.

On June 27, before the standard pre-match press conference ahead of the quarterfinal against France, before any questions were taken, Rapinoe made a statement from the podium.

---

133   @alikrieger, Tweet, June 26, 2019. twitter.com/alikrieger/status /1143941893086162945

With Rapinoe seated next to the communications officer from FIFA and head coach Jill Ellis, the officer invited her to start with a few words, as Ellis smiled ever-so-slightly.

"Obviously, a lot of news recently," Rapinoe said. "I stand by the comments that I made about not wanting to go to the White House—with the exception of the expletive, my mom will be very upset about that."

Rapinoe once again grappled with the idea that her platform, and the team's platform, could be shared by the current administration. She didn't even consider it sharing, not really, but was concerned that it would be co-opted, and that she and the rest of the team would lose control over any encounter. At the end of the day, she viewed herself and the team as fighting for completely opposite things as the President.

She then politely brushed aside the possibility of any follow-up questions on this front, preferring the standard mix of soccer-related inquiries ahead of the quarterfinal. The next day, she accepted an invitation from New York Representative Alexandria Ocasio-Cortez to tour the House of Representatives (extended to her and the rest of the national team, with a tongue-in-cheek note that it "may not be the White House"[134]) via Twitter.

Of course, Rapinoe would go on to score both goals in that game against France, sending the United States on to Lyon for a semifinal against England. With all the

---

134 @AOC, Tweet, June 28, 2019. twitter.com/AOC/status /1144739914384367617

pressure on and off the field, Rapinoe performed once again.

Her partner, Sue Bird, wrote her own take on events in a story for *The Players' Tribune* posted ahead of the World Cup semifinals—a story titled, "So the President F-cking Hates My Girlfriend."

Bird wrote that while she shared the same political beliefs as Rapinoe, their approaches generally could not be more different—and in fact, she was scared in many ways by the very public nature of the dispute between Rapinoe and Trump, and his followers.

That said, there was also a surrealness to it—that the President of the United States was tweeting about her girlfriend. "It would be ridiculous to the point of laughter, if it wasn't so gross," Bird wrote, with an aside that reminded her readers that Trump's political agenda was also "ruining the lives of so many innocent people."[135]

But there was legitimate fear as well, not just for Rapinoe's sake, but for Bird and Krieger and other figures who were publicly supporting and close to her as well. As Bird wrote, the fight didn't end on Twitter. Fox News featured segments on Rapinoe on a regular basis; the fight had consumed more than just some hostile

135 Bird, Sue. "So the President F*cking Hates My Girlfriend," *The Players' Tribune*, July 2, 2019. www.theplayerstribune.com/en-us/articles/sue-bird-megan-rapinoe-uswnt

people on the Internet, it was making headlines across the country.

But from Bird's viewpoint—who had watched Rapinoe's evolution over the past few years up close and personal—the entire incident simply reinforced her character, the lessons she already learned. That in fact, the way Rapinoe handled a strange standoff with the President was only possible because of what she previously lived through, the consequences she already saw in 2016, 2017, and 2018 after kneeling during the anthem. While constrained by US Soccer's rules on how she could continue her protest, it only strengthened her resolve to continue in new ways.

As Bird wrote, Rapinoe was unflappable (at least externally) and unapologetic. Bird knew this wasn't an act, that Rapinoe both knew what she was about as a human, and that she carried herself with confidence. Even as she was sensitive to public perception of herself, Bird knew that her partner could also use that sensitivity to her own advantage—and to, as she had tirelessly advocated for so long—see outside of herself. To do better.

Bird wasn't suggesting in her article that Rapinoe was centering herself in this fight, merely that the fight had shown her true character as an ally. "The Megan you're seeing at this World Cup?" Bird asked, "it's an even stronger version of the one who knelt in the first place."[136]

---

136 Ibid.

While Rapinoe did her best to keep the focus on the USA vs. France quarterfinal, she ended up not playing in the semifinal against England thanks to a hamstring injury. After a nervy win over the Lionesses, there were another five days until the United States would play again in the championship match. The wait included one of the tournament's rare days off, a full rest day for the remaining teams ahead of the third-place match and final.

That rest day happened to be the Fourth of July.

But before the rest day, the US national team was on the hook for their regular media availability. With the upcoming American holiday clearly in mind, Rapinoe was asked about the very concept of patriotism, how it applied to her. By then, it was eight days after the video went viral, and she used the time to reflect once again on her journey.

"I think that I'm particularly and uniquely and very deeply American," she answered. "If we want to talk about the ideals that we stand for, the song and the anthem, and what we were founded on—I think I'm extremely American."

She also had a message for those who expressed disappointment at her methods, who bombarded her mentions, who photoshopped "Make America Great Again" flags into her hand in photographs from the World Cup.

"I would have them look hard into what I'm actually saying, the actions that I'm doing," she said. After all, she was more than willing to be a part of a larger discussion about which methods were productive, and which weren't.

"I know that I'm not perfect," she said. "But I think that I stand for honesty and for truth and for wanting to have the conversation. Looking at the country honestly and saying, yes, we are a great country, and there are many things that are so amazing and I feel very fortunate to be in this country. I would never be able to do this in a lot of other places."

She returned to one of her most common motifs: the concept that we, as a people, and we, as a nation, could simply do better. That there was clearly room for improvement for all citizens, not just the ones that agreed with her.

"It doesn't mean that we shouldn't always strive to be better," she said. "I think that this country was founded on a lot of good ideals, but it was also founded on slavery. And I think we just need to be really honest about that, and be really open in talking about that so we can reconcile that and hopefully move forward and make this country better for everyone."

Those quotes would drive another full news cycle during the World Cup. As usual, they proved to be divisive, with Rapinoe's detractors particularly taking offense to the concept that the practice of slavery may have played a role in the nation's founding. But she also found support. Columnist Nancy Armour of *USA Today*, for instance, went all in on Rapinoe's critics, calling them out for not understanding the fundamental concept of patriotism.

Rapinoe's critics, for Armour, did not actually want to put in the work to make a more perfect union, but allow a flawed nation to benefit only a few. "America is not easy," Armour wrote. "At least, it's not supposed to be. Megan Rapinoe gets that. The question, as this country prepares to celebrate its independence, is why so many of her detractors do not."[137]

Four days later, the United States went on to win the World Cup over the Netherlands, thanks in part to a Megan Rapinoe goal.

A few weeks later, with the tournament behind her—and the days-long celebrations behind her as well—Rapinoe was able to assess the entire situation with some distance in an interview with *The Guardian*, calling it "ridiculous and absurd."[138]

She was only concerned how it could have affected the team on the field; she set aside any concerns about herself. As much as Sue Bird found the conflict baffling but still scary, Rapinoe only found it baffling to be in a Twitter fight with Trump.

---

137   Armour, Nancy. "Opinion: USWNT's Megan Rapinoe is living her patriotism at World Cup. What's your excuse?" *USA Today*, July 3, 2019. www.usatoday.com/story/sports/columnist/nancy -armour/2019/07/03/world-cup-2019-megan-rapinoe-more -american-those-criticize-her/1641234001/
138   Brockes, Emma. "Megan Rapinoe: 'We're everything Trump loves—except that we're powerful women,'" *The Guardian*, August 17, 2019. www.theguardian.com/football/2019/aug/17/megan-rapinoe -everything-trump-loves-except-we-are-powerful-women

"People were like: 'That was so intense!' And I'm like: 'Honestly, he's a fucking joke, so it wasn't intense, because this is ridiculous.'"[139]

She also learned one very important lesson from the events of 2016: never read the comments.

"I never have," she said. "And I think I'd been conditioned, from kneeling, to being used to the craziest shit happening in my Twitter feed."[140]

Backlash aside, she was still determined to ensure that her messaging stayed her own. In the end, the White House did extend a formal offer for the team to visit, backing up Trump's tweet, but this offer was made in private—as confirmed by US Soccer to *Sports Illustrated*.[141]

Rapinoe told *Sports Illustrated* that she found out about this offer while flying back from France immediately after the tournament ended, directly from US Soccer President Carlos Cordeiro—who thought a trip to both the White House and the House of Representatives via Ocasio-Cortez could provide some sort of compromise. But both Rapinoe and another player refused any meetings with Trump—still concerned about their platform being co-opted by any public appearance with him.

Rapinoe and the rest of the US national team never went to the White House. But she'd still like to make

---

139   Ibid.

140   Ibid.

141   Vrentas, Jenny. "2019 Sportsperson of the Year: Megan Rapinoe," *Sports Illustrated*, December 9, 2019. www.si.com /sportsperson/2019/12/09/megan-rapinoe-2019-sportsperson -of-the-year

that visit to the House of Representatives work with her and the team's schedule, even as she expressed her doubts to *Sports Illustrated* that US Soccer would organize a trip that skips a presidential meeting.

She found other avenues to flex her new political might though, outside of trips to Washington, DC.

First, she signed on to be a co-chair of Michelle Obama's non-profit and nonpartisan voting participation drive, "When We All Vote." The message of the organization was one that Rapinoe could have written herself: "We're helping bring even more people into the voting process because when we all vote, we all do better."[142]

Fellow co-chairs included public figures such as Lin-Manuel Miranda, Shonda Rhimes, Tom Hanks, Selena Gomez, the list went on.

"Voting is our duty as citizens," Rapinoe said in an interview about why she joined up with Obama. "I want my voice to be heard, I want to be an active participant, and I want to have a say in the country I live in. I believe we can ALL have a better life, but in order to do so, we need people in office who will fight for us ALL."[143]

142 "About Us," When We Vote. www.whenweallvote.org/about-us/
143 Feller, Madison. "Selena Gomez, Megan Rapinoe, Janelle Monáe, And More Partner Up With Michelle Obama To Increase Voter Participation," *Elle Magazine*, November 7, 2019. www.elle.com /culture/career-politics/a29723157/michelle-obama-when-we-all -vote-selena-gomez-2020/

Working to increase voter participation was step one. Step two was a far more personal decision.

By the end of the year, she was comfortable enough to endorse a candidate for president. In December, she released a video endorsing Elizabeth Warren's campaign—a video which documented a phone call between Rapinoe and Warren from both sides, in which both expressed admiration from the other.

"You have shown such great leadership this year," Warren said to Rapinoe, as shown in the video. "What a remarkable year and what a remarkable week for you. You've just been named Sportsperson of the Year. It's fabulous and well-deserved. And well-deserved because you get out there and you both lead your team on the field, but you also help lead America off the field and that's really important."

Rapinoe went on CNN to explain her endorsement, and Warren's appeal for the issues that mattered most to her.

"I think we need really big, bold, brave progressive policies," she said. "There's a number of things that are happening in the country right now that need to change, and the way I see it, they're all interconnected."[144]

For Rapinoe, that vision was one shared by Warren—one that the candidate expressed via her speeches and

144 Sullivan, Kate and Caroline Kelly. "Megan Rapinoe backs Warren: 'I just feel like I trust her,'" CNN, December 14, 2019. www.cnn.com/2019/12/13/politics/megan-rapinoe-endorses -elizabeth-warren/index.html

policies. She loved Warren's belief that America could listen to everyone's voices, regardless of background. Rapinoe appreciated that Warren had visited places like West Virginia and red-lined communities to find shared challenges—and she didn't hate that Warren wasn't afraid of the 1 percent, telling them that she expected the rich to pay their fair share.

Ultimately, for Rapinoe, it came down to one simple fact. "I just feel like I trust her."[145]

And for someone who lived through a very public battle with Donald Trump earlier in the year, she also stressed that she thought everyone was focused too much on him, and too much on the potential electability of candidates when put up against him.

"Obviously, he's this crazy force that's happening right now, but I also think we need to show people. I think we need to show people that there is another path forward," she said.[146]

And while Rapinoe waited a bit to endorse Warren, likely waiting to see what would come of California Senator Kamala Harris's campaign (as she had attended events in her home state), it did make perfect sense.

At the start of 2020 at an event in New Hampshire before the start of the primaries, Warren was asked a question about how she would make minorities—including LGBTQ people—feel safer in America. Her answer and

---

145 Ibid.
146 Ibid.

her line of thinking overlapped entirely with Rapinoe's entire approach.

"I believe in an America where we can value every single person," Warren answered. "If we do that, that gives us the chance to pick up each other's fights as our own. I've watched during this campaign and been encouraged as straight people have picked up the fight for LGBTQ rights, as men have picked up the fights for women's reproductive rights, as whites have picked up the fight for racial justice, as all of us have picked up the fight for climate change. We can pick up each other's fights. And out of that, knit together respect for each other, and true belief in not an America of the past, but the America of the future we want to be."[147]

As 2020 began, Rapinoe was all in on this vision of the future. Her goal was to "remain hopeful and optimistic knowing that we all have the power to change the world."[148] Rapinoe didn't have this amount of political clout just from one summer. Looking back on all the experiences it took to get her to this specific moment in time, it took her a decade of work—both activism and work on herself—to earn this platform. Before Rapinoe, no presidential candidate looked for an endorsement from a women's soccer player.

147   @deepa_shivaram, Tweet, January 2, 2020. twitter.com/deepa
_shivaram/status/1212888322198188037
148   @mendico, Instagram, January 4, 2020. www.instagram.com/p
/B65924UBd1F/

Warren eventually dropped out of the race, and while Rapinoe felt disappointed, it did not deter her from staying politically active. She refused to stick to sports, and refused to stay in her lane. She realized she had a power and voice in this space, a way to embrace what America meant to her. She could challenge the status quo, without giving up soccer.

Eight years ago, she sang "Born in the U.S.A." into a field mic at the World Cup, using the chorus in celebration without reflecting on the rest of the song. But Bruce Springsteen's anthemic hit is not a celebration, but instead exposes the country's treatment of soldiers and the hypocritical nature of the military-industrial complex—the very thing everyone rushed to defend against Rapinoe's actions in 2016.

Rapinoe still played soccer for the good ol' US of A as 2019 turned to 2020. She still felt particularly and uniquely and deeply American. But her eyes were opened. And above all, she was determined to do better.

CHAPTER TWELVE

Celebrate the wins

"I deserve this."

MEGAN RAPINOE SCORED HER FIRST goal of the 2019 World Cup against Thailand, in the United States' opening game of the tournament. When she scored in the 79th minute of the game, the United States was already up 8–0 over their opponents. She beat the last defender inside the box before pushing the ball past goalkeeper Sukanya Chor Charoenying, who eventually let in a total of thirteen goals before the final whistle.

After Rapinoe got to her feet, she spread her arms in celebration and made a run for the bench—twirling a few times along the way, before diving right in front of the substitutes and kicking up her leg in joy a couple of times. She hopped back up, and was immediately surrounded by her teammates, embraced in a swarm of celebratory hugs.

That same match, Alex Morgan scored five goals of her own, tying a World Cup record for most goals scored in a match, and the United States set a new record for most goals scored by a team in a World Cup match.

Even before the game ended, Rapinoe, Morgan, and the rest of the team were already being questioned for the celebrations during the game, called classless by fans and media, told to act like "they had been there before," especially since they won the 2015 World Cup.

Even as the United States opened their tournament with a massive win, reminding their opponents that they were in fact the team to beat—not just as the defending champions—the 13–0 win turned into a lose-lose scenario when it came to public discourse.

While Morgan scored five goals, Rapinoe and Carli Lloyd one each, four different players also scored their first World Cup goals ever, in Sam Mewis, Lindsey Horan, Mal Pugh, and Rose Lavelle. The World Cup is also the signature event of the sport, with a four-year cycle of building and qualifications; which also meant four years of sacrifice and work for every single player who was on the roster. On that same note, had the USWNT batted the ball around the field and avoided scoring on Thailand for an entire half, they also would have been criticized by the public.

"This is a world championship," head coach Jill Ellis said in the postgame press conference. "Every team that's here has been fantastic to get to this point. To be respectful to an opponent is to play hard against an opponent."

Morgan also reminded the media in the mixed zone that those celebrations said nothing about Thailand and their quality as a team. "I think it was important for us to celebrate with each other," she said.

The next day, Rapinoe appeared on television to further address the negative reactions, telling FOX Soccer reporter Alex Curry that she saw some of the blowback already.[149]

First, she reminded the viewers that four of the team's goalscorers did so in their World Cup debuts and were not on the team during the 2015 win.

"I understand it in part, but honestly, first of all, this is the World Cup," she said. "This is something that Lindsey (Horan) and Sam (Mewis) and Rose (Lavelle) and Mal (Pugh), they've been dreaming about for their whole lives. So you can't fault them for that joy."

But she also rejected the implications that the team did anything wrong, that their behavior disrespected the game. In her mind, the team's only crime was joy, which was no crime at all.

She pointed to the months leading up the tournament, essentially bringing up the lawsuit against the federation without having to mention it by name. But fundamentally, the opening match of the tournament was only about the emotions from the team, for the team;

---

149   FOX Sports live programming, Women's World Cup, June 12, 2019.

the joy being shared by every single player on the pitch and on the bench, together.

There has been a strange tradition of condemning success on the women's side of the game, and not just limited to women's soccer. The United States national team was now in that same space occupied by the University of Connecticut women's basketball team, who were deemed bad for the game because of their dynastic success. The USA women's basketball national team was in this mix too, along with both USA and Canada in women's hockey.

For all of these teams, it was a damned if you do, damned if you don't. Win—and worse yet, celebrate those wins—and you're bad for the game. Take it easy on an opponent, and get called out for lack of respect. As expected, there was global hand-wringing over the 13–0 game between the United States and Thailand, with much less attention focused on why such a disparity between two qualified teams would exist at the most important tournament, and much more focused on how this was a poor example from the role models of women's soccer.

The next day, Rapinoe rolled into FOX Soccer's Paris set in a leather jacket for some interview time alongside Alex Morgan, during which she revealed her celebration was actually a direct shout-out to her friend and the team's back-up goalkeeper, Ashlyn Harris.

She also said that her decision to celebrate her goal in such a fashion was made in the moment.

"Obviously, we have the utmost respect for all of the opponents that we play, and we'll continue to do so, forever and ever," she said. She brought up what she said the day before, about joy that was involved. "That sort of explosion of joy was very genuine for us."[150]

The joy wasn't about to end either, even as the scorelines did get much closer. By the time the knock-out stages rolled around, it took Megan Rapinoe scoring two penalty kicks to move past Spain in a nervy round-of-16 match. Rapinoe would prove clutch again during the quarterfinal against host nation France in Paris. She also made the World Cup debut of what would become her iconic celebration pose during that quarterfinal—arms outstretched, chest raised, chin up, a dare and an invitation all at the same time.

She actually previewed the celebration on American shores, before the tournament even started. Rapinoe always was one of the more exuberant on the team during celebrations—and always willing to take a flying leap into the arms of a teammate. But this deliberate pose was something new, and most didn't even notice it as anything particularly special when she pulled it at Red Bull Arena in May 2019.

---

150   FOX Sports live programming, Women's World Cup, June 13, 2019.

The US national team defeated Mexico in the team's final friendly before heading to Europe, but before heading for one last round of media and then the airport, US Soccer arranged a brief send-off ceremony. It was one last bit of pomp and circumstance, complete with fireworks even in the late afternoon sun in New Jersey.

As each player stepped through the arch, being introduced to the American crowd one final time as part of the World Cup roster, some opted for waves, some opted for celebrations. Defender Emily Sonnett went all out, jumping in the air, knowing the team's photographer was at the ready.

Rapinoe stepped through when her name was called, and raised her arms in celebration. It was a gesture she would turn to again, on much larger stages.

After knocking France out of the World Cup, Rapinoe did not play in the semifinal against England due to injury. She did return for the final, and once again, provided the goal that proved to be the game-winner against the Netherlands.

Again, it was a penalty kick that would determine the United States' fate, with Rapinoe over the ball to take it. Morgan took a high kick in the box to earn the foul, but Rapinoe at this point was guaranteed to be the team's choice for penalties.

Rapinoe froze Dutch goalkeeper Sari van Veenendaal with her shot, not placing it in the far corner, but only slightly off center. All van Veenendaal could do was collapse to one knee as the ball passed her, and Rapinoe ran for the corner to celebrate.

She twirled once to check on the progress of her teammates behind her, before facing the crowd to strike the pose. It only took another second before Alex Morgan jumped on her back in celebration, before the rest of the players on the field and the substitutes from the bench all joined into one swarming mass of joy near the corner flag at the stadium in Lyon.

After the match, she revealed that once again, she didn't have a specific plan to turn to the pose before the game. "I don't know, it just feels right for the moment," she said. "I mean, I'm generally pretty off-the-cuff so I change them up a lot, but this just felt right in this moment."

Even if it wasn't planned, Rapinoe was far surer of what she hoped to convey through her celebrations, particularly the now famous pose. She knew exactly what those outstretched arms meant.

"To have me, and the person that I am and the things that I stand for, with a big shit-eating grin on your face, just in all of our glory," she said in the press conference after the final. "I say that as my team, and of all the women's players that have played in this tournament and around the world. I feel like it's kind of iconic of everything we've gone through and continue to go through, and still we put this beautiful product out on the pitch."

She elaborated on that thought later in the evening, while speaking to the mixed zone. The wins and the celebrations were important, because it reinforced everything that she said about the national team, about their purpose beyond the pitch. The goals and the wins made the celebrations possible, but they also meant that Rapinoe and the rest of the team had a much larger platform to work from.

"Obviously getting to play at the highest level at a World Cup with a team like we have is ridiculous," she told the media. "But to be able to couple that with everything off the field, to back up all of those words with performances, and to back up all of those performances with words, it's just incredible. I've said this before, but I feel like this team is in the midst of changing the world around us, as we live. It's an incredible feeling."

The World Cup win didn't just mean that Rapinoe and the other players on the team were going to hold on to the world's attention a little longer, it also meant a party. And the team was absolutely ready to do just that, with what seemed like an endless supply of champagne.

"I live my best life in celebration mode," Rapinoe said, after she eventually survived the week-long party. "My performance in the World Cup was good, but I was thinking all along, 'Just wait until I get to the celebrations.' I love celebrating. We'd been cooped up for 50 days together. To be a team that is expected to win all the time—it's exciting when you do, but it's also this massive relief because it would be a huge letdown if you didn't. Then to win in such spectacular fashion! You get to revel in it for days. You get to do whatever the fuck you want."[151]

USWNT goalkeeper Ashlyn Harris documented the days-long celebration via her Instagram story, from the locker room at the stadium in Lyon, to the night out on the town, then the flight back home through pool parties at a New York City hotel. Even the partying could not escape the discourse, with some opining that the team's language was too foul, they were once again being poor role models between the cursing and the dancing and the sheer amount of beer and champagne they managed to either drink or pour on each other.

The team continued to ignore all of that though. Defender Kelley O'Hara spent the entirety of the ticker-tape parade hoping for someone to toss her a beer, and actually have it work. The champagne was flowing on the floats, and the sunglasses were firmly on.

The party didn't stop in New York, as the team jetted off to Los Angeles to accept an ESPY award in person, but Rapinoe's stand-out moment from Ashlyn Harris's

151   Marchese, David. "Megan Rapinoe is in celebration mode. And she's got some things to say." The *New York Times Magazine*, July 29, 2019. www.nytimes.com/interactive/2019/07/29/magazine /megan-rapinoe-sports-politics.html

200 SECRETS OF SUCCESS

extensive documentation happened in New York City during the parade.

Perched on the trailer bed, with a bottle of champagne in one hand and the World Cup trophy in the other, bright red sunglasses and four-star t-shirt on, she loudly declared to Harris and her phone's camera, "I deserve this."

Harris asked back, "What do you deserve?"

Rapinoe replied, "I deserve this."

"You deserve all of it," Harris said.

"Everything," Rapinoe mouthed.

Those three words—"I deserve this"—quickly turned into both a rallying cry for women inspired by Rapinoe and the United States national team, as well as a meme. GIFs were created of Rapinoe shouting into the camera, and they were quickly put to use for celebrations of the most basic functions of adulthood, then rewarding oneself for that bare minimum.

The *Huffington Post*'s brief article on the video was titled, "Megan Rapinoe Holding World Cup Trophy And Screaming 'I Deserve This' Is A Mood" with writer Jenna Amatulli declared that Rapinoe had given everyone a "mantra we need."[152]

The day after the ticker-tape parade in New York City, the headline on the back cover of the *New York Daily News* read, in giant block letters over a photo of

---

152   Amatulli, Jenna. "Megan Rapinoe Holding World Cup Trophy And Screaming 'I Deserve This' Is A Mood," *Huffington Post*, July 10, 2019. www.huffpost.com/entry/megan-rapinoe-i-deserve-this-ashlyn-harris-womens-soccer_n_5d26016de4b0583e482a870a

Rapinoe and the team celebrating, "MEGAN AMERICA GREAT."

Once again, for as much as the general reaction was positive, there was of course additional backlash over even this. And again, the reaction tended to break down into a gendered response—women felt empowered by Rapinoe claiming her reward, but some men found it selfish.

None of the reaction, regardless of if it was positive or negative, would have ever actually changed the team's behavior.

The joy didn't end at the World Cup or even with the celebrations immediately following in the locker room or back in America. For as much extra work as it has been for Rapinoe across the back half of 2019 and into 2020, there is clearly something she finds joyful about using her platform. There is a potential to extend the party even further at the 2020 Olympic Games in Tokyo, as well.

Humor has also always been a tool for Rapinoe, in every interview and every speech. She's mastered the art of diffusing the tension in a room, even as she tries to force her audience to confront hard or uncomfortable truths about themselves or their own inaction. She's made jokes at her own expense in order to do this; she's shared her own journey and her own vulnerability. Her sense of humor is simply a part of who she is, but it has also given her an edge in how she relates to the world at large.

Rapinoe and the United States national team won the World Cup. They celebrated every step of the way. They serve as a reminder that it's okay to have joy, to aggressively take up space, to know what you deserve.

CONCLUSION

"Caring is cool."

ALL OF THE PILLARS THAT define Megan Rapinoe's success need just one ingredient: for privilege to be erased, for power to be redefined, for platforms to be shared, for people to buy into the idea of collective action, people have to care. They must take that first step from witnessing and understanding to action itself.

In Rapinoe's world, you can't be afraid. You can't be selfish and try to ensure that you still end up with power or resources others don't have access to. If you improve your community, you benefit. If you look out for yourself first, if you buy into the idea that scarcity rules, the whole thing falls apart.

204 • SECRETS OF SUCCESS

"I don't want to live in that kind of world," she said. "I don't think that kind of world is the world that suits everybody, and is going to move us forward in the direction that we need to go."

Rapinoe wants people to change the narrative, to reframe kindness as valuable.

"Caring is cool, right?" she asked, during one of her speeches. "Lending your platform to others is cool. Sharing your knowledge and your success and your influence and your power is cool.

"Giving—" and here Rapinoe paused for a second before continuing, as surrounding her on the stage were youth players, a wrinkle she hadn't expected for this particular part of her speech. "I didn't know the kids were going to be here," she joked, before pressing on. "But giving all of the fucks is cool, you know? Doing more is cool."

Rapinoe's primary image of herself has always been built around the concept of coolness—regardless of how a brand or team or league may have tried to box her into a typical women's soccer image of a responsible role model. Bringing the concept of caring about one's community into that idea of coolness, was, in some ways, simply a new (and cooler) form of being a role model, but one that she could own in her own way.

She didn't push back against additional responsibility, even if it was, to some extent, unfair. The male players she has called out aren't expected to be role models in the same way, aren't expected to carry the success of an entire sport on their shoulders. They show up and play soccer. But Rapinoe has embraced those responsibilities and used them to increase her reach and expand her message.

She's just waiting for more people to catch up.

The secrets of Megan Rapinoe's success are simple and can be enacted in ways both small and large. Not everyone is going to have the volume, the platform, the ability to walk into a room with the most powerful people in their industry. But you can scale down that same approach, and figure out what works best for your neighborhood, your community, or an issue you care strongly about.

These twelve pillars rely on your values and your commitment to your community:

The journey will shape you, but never forget where you came from and your fundamental values. You might outgrow your hometown, your family might end up with different political beliefs, but you're still shaped by your community. It might just prove that your eyes are opened once you leave it.

Be authentic to who you are, even when it's tough. Staying true to your values isn't easy all the time. But when you're challenged, revisit what makes you the best version of yourself to find a solution.

Let your identity guide you. Even as you know the forces and values that shaped you, you also have to be comfortable and confident with yourself.

Your identity and your values must result in solidarity and allyship. Once you know yourself and your relationship with your community, use that knowledge to understand what others are going through. You can't just look out for yourself, you need to step in for people who need help. In return, they will help you.

Know your worth. If others don't see it, take matters into your own hands. If people doubt what you contribute, show them why they're wrong. You might have to color outside the lines, but carve a space for yourself and own how you want to be presented to the world.

Stand your ground on equality, always. There are some things that aren't up for debate. Never stop fighting to ensure that you and others have the full rights and abilities of everyone else in your community.

You must do your part to change the world around you. No matter the scale, you can do your part to improve things for your community. Start small, get others involved. All these actions add up, but it takes you and those around you to buy into this system.

Demand accountability from those with power. If powerful people in your community aren't helping, hold their feet to the fire. Make them witnesses; figure out ways that they could contribute their efforts, and specify that information. Publically.

Use your privilege to lift others up. Throw down your ladders. Share your platform with others who struggle to be heard. There's no risk here, only reward as you get stronger. You can lose alone, or win together.

Grant recognition to those who paved the way, and let them help show you the way forward. Know who came before you, to give yourself the context of how much work has been done already, and what work you can do next. Build upon the previous generations, without forgetting their contributions.

Don't listen when people tell you to stay in your lane. Whatever your version of "stick to sports" is, ignore it. Get involved in community efforts and politics when they directly affect you and those in your community. Be ready to stand up for yourself and others.

Celebrate the wins. Never, ever forget to have fun along the way. Don't let others police your behavior. There is always space for joy, even when it gets frustrating.

So, in the words of Megan Rapinoe, are you ready to do more? Are you ready to do what you can? Are you ready to step outside yourself?

"Be more. Be better. Be bigger than you've ever been before."

Acknowledgments

To my wife, Marjorie—who I once roped into recording an hour-long podcast on Megan Rapinoe while we were both holed up in an Airbnb without air-conditioning in Lyon ahead of the World Cup final, despite her not really being a sports person—she has supported me through a couple of the twists and turns of being one of the rare full-time women's soccer writers, and more specifically through the writing of this book, thank you. Thank you for volunteering to transcribe the interviews that didn't actually talk about the game of soccer, as well. And thanks to DeWitt, who offered endless emotional support.

To the crew at *The Athletic*, thanks for an incredible year, filled with a lot of travel, a lot of articles, and a lot of Slack messages. Thank you for believing in covering women's soccer the way it deserves to be covered.

To all those who watch women's soccer, to those who might start soon, and particularly those who have read my work in some form or another over the past decade— thank you for your support.

And to Pinoe, keep talking. I promise to be around as long as I can with a recorder in hand, to keep telling these stories and truths that need to be told. Thank you for unknowingly defining so much of my career.